Mastership and Understanding of Life

KING SOLOMON SPIRITUAL LIBRARY
THE GOD ENCYCLOPAEDIA WORD OF INFINITY

BY
THE SPIRIT OF THE FATHER GOD
THROUGH HIS SERVANT
HRM KING SOLOMON DAVID JESSE ETE
(King Solomon Spiritual Library)
Eteroyal Universal Family - BCS

All rights reserved
Copyright © Solomon ETE, 2008
Solomon ETE is hereby identified as author of this work in accordance with Section 77 of the Copyright, Designs and Patents Act 1988

The book cover picture is copyright to Solomon ETE

This book is published by
King Solomon Spiritual Library
P O BOX 27394
London E12 6WW UK
www.ksslibrary.com
www.kingsolomonspirituallibrary.com

This book is sold subject to the conditions that it shall not, by way of trade or otherwise, be lent, resold, hired out or otherwise circulated without the author's or publisher's prior consent in any form of binding or cover other than that in which it is published and without a similar condition including this condition being imposed on the subsequent purchaser.

A CIP record for this book is available from the British Library
ISBN 978-0-9559801-7-6

THE MASTERSHIP

THE UNDERSTANDING OF LIFE

Contents

CHAPTER ONE   *11-74*
MASTERSHIP

CHAPTER TWO   *75-196*
THE UNDERSTANDING OF LIFE

THE KEYS

Part One   *80-114*
SPIRITUAL COMMUNICATION

Key A: Planetary Origin
Key B: Evolution and Transit of birth
Key C: Meeting Point
Key D: Right Meeting
Key E: Wrong Meeting

Part Two   *114-152*
MIXING RIGHT AND WRONG TEMPLATE

Key A: Evolution of Nature and Improvement
Key B: Wrong contact Address
Key C: Missing the Point
Key D: Wrong Choice
Key E: Frustration
Key F: Make wrong Commitment
Key G: The Confusion Stage
Key H: The Cause, Effect and Matter

Part Three   *152-160*
THE REMEDY

Key A: The School of the Lower Self Primary; Seven Tests of Brotherhood
Key B: School of Experience, The Secondary Test of Brotherhood: from Cross to Love
Key C: The School of Higher Self; To Acquire the Stage of Indestructible Five Star

Part Four 160-182
UNDERSTANDING OF LIFE

Key A: Higher Consciousness of Life and Self Awareness
Key B: Man know thyself and ye shall pass all Test
Key C: The Right Communication
Key D: The Right Choice
Key E: Correction of Error
Key F: The next Meeting at the Right Address
Key G: Finding Your Other Halt
Key H: Corporation with Your Other Selves, Your Souls Object of Creation

Part Five 182-196
CONCLUSION: MEANINGFUL LIFE

Key A: The meaning of Life
Key B: Identification with the Original Sibling

Key C: Either Human-God or Human-Animal

Key D: Image and Likeness of Good Nature

Key E: Ability to save Other Souls (Helper and Servant of The Holy Spirit)

Key F: AMFAR- ONE Brosisco

Key G: GOD PRESENT!

CHAPTER THREE   197-239
THE INSPIRATIONAL WRITERS

Mastership and Understanding of Life

Chapter one

MASTERSHIP
"THE TOTAL YOU"
(WISDOM, UNDERSTANDING AND KNOWLEDGE)

Mastership and Understanding of Life

FATHER'S TALK (GOD PRESENT)

DATE: BC/AA/BOOC (Twenty-Third November Two Thousand and Four)

In the name of Our Lord Jesus Christ
In the Blood of Our Lord Jesus Christ
Now and forever more

Today! It pleases **ME THE FATHER GOD THE CREATOR OF THE UNIVERSE** to give this Lecture Revelation titled, **THE MASTERSHIP "THE TOTAL YOU" (WISDOM, UNDERSTANDING AND KNOWLEDGE)**

THE SELF COMPONENTS

Man is the **MASTER** of himself. If you are not a **MASTER** of yourself that means that you are slave to yourself. When you are slave to yourself, you cannot represent **ME,** no-way, where can you do that?

Nowhere! That is why **I** have to send preachers, one after the other to come and preach to you people asking you to behave properly, because you are babies. You are slaves and servants to yourself. The reason that a lot of people do a lot of negative things is because they are slaves to themselves. Do you know '**SELF**', as yourself? '**SELF**' has so many components. As '**SELF**' is in the **PHYSICAL SYSTEM** so also it is in the **SPIRITUAL SYSTEM**. The **SOUL** is and has one **SELF** but that **SELF** consists of so many components. In the **PHYSICAL SELF**, the components of one person consist of the **HEART, HEAD,** and the **BRAIN**. The **BRAIN** is in the **HEAD** and the **MIND** is in the **HEART**. The **TONGUE** is the **HYPHEN**. Words come out from the **MOUTH** as the end result of thoughts which are spoken by the **TONGUE** in the **MOUTH**.

Also in the **PHYSICAL BODY,** components starting from the **HEAD,** which has four major parts namely, the **EYES,** the **EARS** the **NOSE** and the **MOUTH.** The **EYES** are to see, the **EAR** is for hearing, **NOSE** is to breathe and smell and the **MOUTH** is for talking and eating. These parts also have their components. An **EYE** has the eyeballs for blinking and the eyelashes for filtering. The **EARS** has earlobes for filtering the ear. The **NOSE** has two nostrils for support and beauty. The **MOUTH** has the tongue for talking and tasting and the teeth for chewing. Other components of the body are, the **HANDS** to touch, **LEGS** to walk with and to move about.

The **STOMACH** harbours food and other abdominal system as a whole. The **BLOOD CELLS** have their stream of blood cells. **FINGERS** for fishing around, finger fingering and touching things. You can see that even hands have their components, which are **FINGERS** and

FINGERS have their components which are nails for scratching. Most of these components are in twos. In actuality, there is only one component in a part, but **THE FATHER GOD** made them in twos for beauty and to support each other. That is why everything must be in two. Brother and sister, father and mother, two eyes, two ears, two hands, two legs and so on. These entire components make up the system which is '**SELF**'.

Every component in the body belongs to a particular body called **MAN**. Are you a man? When the question is asked thus; are you a man, or are you a human being or a person, it is tantamount to asking whether you are a **WHOLE SYSTEM**. Do you have a heart that controls you? Where your mind controls you, you are slave. If your legs control you, that makes you a slave too. If any part of a person's components controls him or her, it makes the person a slave to him or her **SELF**. The human **SELF** is partially divided into two capacities. One is the **SPIRITUAL SELF** and the other is the **PHYSICAL SELF** and both the **SPIRIT** and the **PHYSICAL** must agree in one to make a **MASTER**.

The **MASTER** to **SELF** means that to be a **MASTER** to yourself should not be via your **MIND**. If your **MIND** becomes a **MASTER** carnally, you will make a lot of mistakes because you take action on any thought that occurs to you. It depicts the behavioural pattern of one who is demented, a sick person, one who is mad. In effect, when a person becomes mad, it is because the **MIND** is controlling the person. That is what happens when it said that someone has gone mad. 'Oh, he is mad o' people would say. Anything that the **MIND** says to the person to do or say, he or she does or says it. That shows the person has no control. He has lost control of the system.

MADNESS IS FROM THE MIND NOT FROM THE BRAIN

When somebody goes mad, it is not the brain that malfunctions, it is the **MIND** that has lost control and every system in the body is misled. Sometimes, the **MIND** decides to go forwards and backwards, jumping and singing or laughing and sleeping on the road or picking things from the garbage and eating them and generally displaying all sorts of abnormal behaviours. The person has lost control because the **MASTER** has left the house. The **ACTUAL POSITIVE MASTER** of a person is supposed to be **SELF** because **SELF MEANS THE TOTAL YOU** as **WISDOM, UNDERSTANDING AND KNOWLEDGE**.

WISDOM is the **MASTER** of **HIMSELF** and it is an **INVISIBLE POWER**. When you have, **WISDOM** based in, the **HEART UNDERSTANDING** becomes one with

WISDOM then you have the **MASTER DEGREE**. The **HEART** is the harbour of **THE FATHER'S HIGHER SELF** whilst the mind is the harbour of the lower **SELF.** It is said, 'man knows thyself, and you shall know all things'. If you know yourself then your spiritual eyes are open, your ears are open, your hands become controlled, and your legs become comport.

CORPORATE BOARD OF THE COMPONENTS

The spirit called **WISDOM,** together in oneness with **UNDERSTANDING** manages every part of your body. However, **WISDOM** can operate alone, **UNDERSTANDING** can operate alone, and **KNOWLEDGE** can operate alone. Any power can operate separately with their independent attitudes of pride and arrogance reigning among them. The result of such independent attitude is disagreement and discord. Hence, for a harmonious coexistence, all these powers have to come together with **UNDERSTANDING** to form a corporate board. In this board, they will have a **CHAIRMAN** who will control them and also the **SECRETARY.** <u>**WISDOM** must be the **CHAIRMAN** and the **SECRETARY** becomes **UNDERSTANDING.**</u> With that, every component in your **SPIRITUAL** and **PHYSICAL** body agrees in one, then you become a planned person, a developed person, an **UNDERSTANDABLE** person, and a **GENTLEMAN/WOMAN** and that is the actual meaning of a **GENTLEMAN/WOMAN,** THE PROPER AND ARRANGED PERSON.

When you become a gentleman, and a personality it means that you are a reasonable person. <u>Then **WISDOM** and **UNDERSTANDING** are given glory. People would say, 'Oh, that man or woman is a very **UNDERSTANDABLE** person. 'That man or woman has **WISDOM** and that means that the</u>

CHAIRMAN and the **SECRETARY** are reigning. So when somebody becomes like that in the real sense, he becomes **MY** friend, he is God. That is when **I** can be proud that **I** created that person in **MY** image and likeness. Of the **CHAIRMAN** and the **SECRETARY**, the **SECRETARY** is the **SERVANT**. Any time **I** refer to **SECRETARY**, it means **SERVANT**, somebody who keeps records and does what **I** want. People do not know that the meaning of **SECRETARY** is **SERVANT** of the **CHAIRMAN**.

SECRETARY and **CHAIRMAN** can become friends and when that happens, the company becomes very nice. So you *Disem* are a friend to Brother Solomon, is that right? *'Yes Father.'* And you are his **SECRETARY** because King Solomon David Jesse **ETE** is **MY SECRETARY**. King Solomon is **MY SECRETARY** because **I** pass through him to give all this **WISDOM**. Is it not secretarial work? He is **MY** servant. Therefore anybody who has reached this stage is a **MASTER** of him or her **SELF** and becomes **THE FATHER'S REPRESENTATIVE, THE KEY OF LIFE HOLDER (THE SCHOOL OF HIGHER SELF PROPRIETOR) THE INSPIRATIONAL HEAD AND INJECTOR OF RE-ARRANGED MAN, FRUITION AND FUNCTIONS**

People go about calling people **FATHER'S REPRESENTATIVE! FATHER'S REPRESENTATIVE** and it makes **ME** laugh. Is it **THE FATHER'S** representative in eating *garri* and *eba*? **THE FATHER'S** representative for what? Without **UNDERSTANDING,** can you know yourself? How can you be **MY** representative when you don't know yourself? Do you think **I** do not know **MYSELF**? Ha! Ha! Ha! Ha! Oh *owo!* Of all that **I** created *owo* (human being) is the most difficult. **MY** development of their mental attitude is like training a baby. Tell him or her to 'stay here and don't move'. He or she will react within a second of the instruction and start throwing their legs up and down. They can't help their behaviour, as it is a childish attitude as stupidity. They behave, as they do not know because children behave, as they do not know themselves. When he or she grows up and becomes aware that throwing their legs up and down means they are exposing their privacy, they become shy and behave themselves. As a grown up, you will never tell that person to close his or her legs again because they behave as they know.

This Lecture Revelation is deep because it is the key of life. The key of life that **I AM** giving you is the '**SCHOOL OF THE HIGHER-SELF**' which **I** have been talking about, but people do not seem to comprehend. The '**SCHOOL OF THE HIGHER SELF**' is the **BROTHERHOOD MASTERSHIP** physically therefore, if you come into this world and do not reach this stage of **BROTHERHOOD MASTERSHIP**, you are causing confusion.

The appropriate behaviour of brothers and sisters of the Kingdom is the expected criterion on which **MY** Kingdom is to be firmly established and well rooted so as to engulf the entire humanity. Brothers and sisters must be **MASTERS**. When it is said Brotherhood of the Cross and Star, it means the New Kingdom of God on earth and the majority of brothers and sisters in the Kingdom must be **MASTERS.** Without they being **MASTERS,** do you not see confusion, fighting, quarrelling, and argument with people doing one thing or the other wrongly thinking that they are right?

When young children do certain things which are wrong, they think they are right. If you ask them not to do that, they will say that they have to because they know it to be right. Does a child know anything? They are headstrong. Any time you say to a child, 'do not go to that side'. The child will say, 'no, I have to go to that side, because that is what I want to do.' That is how people who are not **MASTERS** to themselves behave. They behave very stupidly but when you call them stupid, they become annoyed. It is not that you are insulting or abusing them. It means that the person is stupid in the sense that he or she is a baby. Is that understood?

Our Lord Jesus Christ said to the Jews, 'you people are very stupid, because you behave as you do not know,' and they became annoyed. He said to them, 'if you accept that you are stupid, **I** will teach you, but since you people think yourselves to be **MASTERS**, you continue to be stupid'.

BE MASTER OF YOURSELF

When you see somebody who is close to himself, nobody will tell you that this person is comport. He is an arranged person, a **MASTER** in the making. He is somebody who is on the way to being a **MASTER,** knowingly or unknowingly. Some people are naturally **MASTERS** to themselves. They do not join any secret society and do not belong to any

Mastership and Understanding of Life

elementary set ups. They are not involved in anything that propelled them to that status. They are simply **MASTERS.** That is, they are born as an arranged person, a senior person in nature. The more you come to the world and have experience, the more your soul becomes arranged.

Some children are born as arranged persons, but this physical aspect of being a **MASTER** requires being taught. You are an arranged woman. *THE FATHER referring to Queen Disem.* You are not an ordinary woman who is just like that. Nonetheless, if you come and the key is not there and also without the door, you will not become comport to yourself and **I** won't put you in this school. You still do wrong things, but in-between doing the wrong things, you know that it is wrong, yet you still do it. This is because you can't help yourself. You are not able to help yourself for the simple reason that you are not a **MASTER** to yourself, but you are already an arranged person. It can take you a whole year to make a single small decision for yourself, and the more you wait and cannot make a decision, the more mistakes you make. It is because you are not yet matured enough to make quick decisions.

When a judge does not have a clue about a case, he keeps adjourning the case to buy time to gain more **UNDERSTANDING** of the case. From the time, the file and the facts fall into his hands, and he assimilates the information and becomes a **MASTER** of the case then he can make absolute decisions about the case. Therefore, the first and foremost thing required before **I** give anybody any post in this kingdom is that you must have Brotherhood **MASTERSHIP**. That is all that **I** want. **MASTERSHIP** of
Brotherhood means to be a **MASTER** of yourself in your own nature, because **I** did not create man to live according to another person's directive. **I** created man to be autonomous, but to coordinate with others, because every single positive

person is God, **MY REPRESENTATIVE**. In effect, you do not need to use someone else's eyes to see. Some people live their lives by talking about other people because they are using somebody's mouth. They use other people's eyes and voice's, they use other people's hands, and therefore they are borrowers. Borrowers cannot see anything pertaining to themselves; they can only see things about other people. These are gossips and they cause trouble and confusion everywhere.

Is this **WISDOM** from man? *'No Father,' responds Queen Disem.* Is this revelation this morning from a human being? *'No Father'.* King Solomon's **WISDOM**, King Solomon's **WISDOM**, show **ME** King Solomon's **WISDOM! I AM THE WISDOM MYSELF. I** made Him a **MASTER**. You cannot be a King just like that. People cannot make Kings just like that. Look at their faces as if they want to be King. Are you a **MASTER**? Can you make decisions? When you make decisions, are they not wrong? Some people allow their hands to make decisions for them and their hands will touch and touch everything. They use their minds and their mouth to make decisions and talk at random and all they say is negativism and rubbish, because they cannot control their mouth.

When you become a **MASTER** of yourself, **UNDERSTANDING** and **WISDOM** rule and then the still voice is **THE FATHER GOD** in your heart operating coherently. From today, **I** make you, *Queen Disem Solomon David* **ETE** a **MASTER** of yourself. **I** make **MY** positive children **MASTERS**. King Solomon David Jesse **ETE** is already a **MASTER** and has been for ages and **I** make him a **HIGHERSELF MASTER**. A **HIGHERSELF MASTER** is one with **ME THE FATHER GOD** just as His Father Adam, The King of Kings and The Lord of Lords, **AMFAR-ONE, I AND MY FATHER ARE ONE.** Now he is going for **PHD**, while you are doing your **MASTERS.** That is why he is your higher self. **PHD** means **INVISIBLE AND VISIBLE SELF OF THE DIGITAL AGE, THE AGE OF PERFECTION OF LOVE.**

PEACE of **THE FATHER! EMEM ETE! GRACE** of **THE FATHER! MERCY** of **THE FATHER! TRUTH** of **THE FATHER! POWER** of **THE FATHER! ETE** Royal Universal Family will have all that. They have **COMFORT** of **THE FATHER!** And **JOY** of **THE FATHER!**

A SECRET NATION

I AM a good **MASTER** in King Solomon not **MASTER** for rubbish. People say that 'King Solomon David Jesse **ETE** is in a secret society' but he is not; **I AM** the one who created an open society of supreme wisdom for him. His Open Society means THE SUPREME

WISDOM OF THE FATHER GOD as an open **UNDERSTANDING,** but it is the **UNDERSTANDING** that is not common. Anything that is not common is a different society, a different environment, a different location and a different area.

When people do not have access to something they call it a secret society, but for those who have access, to them it is not a secret. So King Solomon David Jesse **ETE** should not be annoyed that they call Him a secret society man. He is for **ME THE FATHER GOD, THE CREATOR OF THE UNIVERSE**. King Solomon David **ETE** Himself is the secret society. In fact, he is a secret Nation; society is too small for him. They should call him Secret Nation. That is another office. Extraordinary man! It is **I** who gave him that title of extraordinary man! Who is an Extraordinary Missionary? Is it not what **I AM** doing at the moment?

Song:
"In the beginning was the word and the Word was God" (repeat two-times)

I can give **UNDERSTANDING** in the morning and in the evening, you replace it with misunderstanding and you become *'stupid'* again. That is what happens when it is said, 'that person does not normally behave like that; He used to behave well.' What transpired in such a situation is that, **I** gave the person **UNDERSTANDING** but the person replaced it with misunderstanding. When the person did not control his or her mind, it is a low nature! You can lose control for one second and in that one second a lot of things can be damaged. That is what makes people say I made a silly mistake. When people say 'I made a silly mistake' and they cannot forgive themselves that is what happened. The person lost control and the **UNDERSTANDING** left, then he or she starts to makes mistakes.

When **I THE FATHER GOD** is with you twenty-four hours, **I** make your mind to be alert. **MY** light is always illuminated and flashing meaning that, The Holy Spirit of **THE FATHER GOD** is switched on and you can never make mistakes. That is why you have to knock your head on the ground. In everything that you do, you should knock your head on the ground to worship and thank **THE FATHER GOD**. In doing that you turn on **THE FATHER, THE CREATOR OF THE UNIVERSE** and it means that you have switched **THE FATHER** on.

King Solomon David Jesse **ETE** is a professor in the **SCHOOL OF THE HIGHER SELF, BROTHERHOOD MASTERSHIP.** That is the work **I** give Him to do. When people call him professor, it is true. He is the one that can arrange a meeting to restore somebody's star that has been spoilt through abortion, because He is working as **MY SECRETARY THE RECORDER** in **MY** office of wisdom that connects to life and soul. Do you **UNDERSTAND** that? *'Yes FATHER'*, *answers Queen Disem.* All these things should be written out without a single thing taken out.

King Solomon David Jesse **ETE** is the only person in the whole universe that **I** give the **UNDERSTANDING** to restore the star of people with the **'code word'**. **I** do this because every human star has a code word, because He is **MY SECRETARY THE MEMORY OF THE FATHER GOD'S SPIRITUAL LIBRARY**. That does not mean that He is the King of Kings and the Lord of Lords. Do you **UNDERSTAND** that? But **I** give Him **UNDERSTANDING** to bring out secret records. **I** give Him the keys. He has seventy two million keys to open the seventy two million positive **SELVES** of **THE FATHER GOD; THE CREATOR OF THE UNIVERSE** and with that, he can help any soul.

When people stop counting sin for King Solomon David Jesse **ETE** and desist from casting blame on Him, stop being jealous of Him and or entertaining any such negative vibes about Him and become close to Him, they would learn one thing or more. And that one thing would be a key to their life. If anybody comes closer to King Solomon David Jesse **ETE** and stops arrogance, being jealous and is in spirit for just one second when **I THE FATHER GOD** start talking or giving a Lecture Revelation through Him and explaining things, the person will acquire at least one key. And that key can help that person in their entire life. If you get one hundred keys then you are a changed community and you are a changed person. **WISDOM, UNDERSTANDING** and **KNOWLEDGE** makes somebody a changed person. People go to school to learn physically to gain **KNOWLEDGE. UNDERSTANDING** works between **WISDOM** and **KNOWLEDGE**.

KNOWLEDGE is **PHYSICAL POWER** whilst **WISDOM** is a **SPIRITUAL POWER. WISDOM** is also the **SPIRITUAL MASTER** and therefore, **WISDOM** is the **CHAIRMAN** of all three.

ACCEPTABLE SYSTEMS IN THE PHYSICAL AND THE SPIRITUAL

The physical **MASTER** next to the **CHAIRMAN** is **KNOWLEDGE**. You can have **WISDOM,** but if you do not go to school and acquire carnal knowledge to gain a degree, masters or a PhD and this and that, the world will not recognize you. Where is your certificate, you are asked? They put you in a low estate. You will not earn a lot of money when you gain employment without appropriate physical certificate. You may know a lot of things naturally, but they must make you attend school through their system and issue you with a certificate. Until you get that degree or that masters or other qualifications, you are not acknowledged. However, when they give that master's degree to you then they recognize you. You can stay at home and they pay you money because in their community, the master's degree is their knowledge. That is why in the system of this world, if you don't join them they won't recognise you through their own understanding, and of their own knowledge. So that degree, that masters certificate, that professorship, that PhD, and that diploma that they give to you makes them to recognize you in their community, in their own way because that constitutes this worlds understanding. Therefore, **UNDERSTANDING** also serves as the **SECRETARY** to the **CHAIRMAN,** the **KNOWLEDGE** in the physical world.

In Spirit, which is **MY** own main part, **I** own both physical and spiritual, which are **THE MOTHER GOD AND THE FATHER GOD,** then **UNDERSTANDING** which is in-between is the child. That is **MY SECRETARY** and the **EXECUTIVE** is also **MY SERVANT**.

Now regarding **WISDOM**, no matter the **KNOWLEDGE** that you posses, if you have no **POWER,** no **PEACE**, no **MERCY**, no **LOVE**, and no **FAITH**, you are nothing to **ME** and in the spirit, you are a baby. If you are a PhD holder here in the world, but you do not have any **POWER** in the spirit, you are less than a baby comparatively in **SPIRITUAL** matters. That is why King Solomon **ETE** – Oh MY SELF! GOD OF HEAVEN AND EARTH! Nobody can be a **MASTER** of himself if he has no **WISDOM** and **KNOWLEDGE,** because with **WISDOM** you should have **KNOWLEDGE.** The reason all the people that have knowledge are making so many mistakes is that they do not have **WISDOM.** You can see that somebody is a holder of a first degree certificate, master's degree, or PhD but he or she is a drunkard. Don't you see that? Is he a **MASTER** of himself? He talks rubbish and can fight over little things. They talk, as they do not know. Lawyers and Judges tell lies and these are against themselves, all in the name of knowledge.

Conclusively, to be **KNOWLEDGEABLE** can never make someone to be a **MASTER** unless there is cooperation with **UNDERSTANDING**. No matter the amount of schools you have attended, no matter the money you have, no matter your power, no matter the visionary you are, no matter your **WISDOM** and the patience you have, in fact anything at all that you may have including beauty, you must have **UNDERSTANDING** with that gift, talent, or ability. The **UNDERSTANDING** will be serving that particular talent then you become a **MASTER** of your gift. That is how you become a personality, and a **MEANINGFUL** person in the community either in spirit or in truth.

THE SIGNATORY TO BROTHERHOOD MASTERSHIP - THE SCHOOL OF HIGHER SELF

The certificate of **BROTHERHOOD MASTERSHIP** from **THE SCHOOL OF THE HIGHER SELF** must have King Solomon David Jesse **ETE'S** signature of recommendation as Incarnated ABEL because He represents **ME** through his Father Adam. He is the only person who can sign that status for people. That was what **I** showed Princess Mfon Etteh some years ago. In a short time, everybody will want HRM KING SOLOMON DAVID JESSE **ETE'S** signature and His Father, **THE KING OF KINGS AND THE LORD OF LORDS** signature as a true servant of Christ. You see? Therefore, **BROTHERHOOD MASTERSHIP** is through "**THE FATHER'S TALK (GOD PRESENT)**" has connections with **MY** preaching.

MY preaching is a way of life. **BROTHERHOOD MASTERSHIP**

"**THE FATHER'S TALK (GOD PRESENT)**" is connects to the gospels of everlasting testimony that King Solomon has been preaching in the altar. When you want to see the **KNOWLEDGE** and **WISDOM** of **THE FATHER GOD**, you should attend bible class. All the Lecture Revelations **I** give in bible class lead to **WISDOM.** They are all **WISDOM.** And **I** give the Holy Spirit to those who read **MY** Lecture Revelations properly to have **UNDERSTANDING.**

When **I** use King Solomon **ETE** to give a Lecture Revelation like this, "THE **FATHER'S TALK (GOD PRESENT)**", it is for the **SCHOOL OF THE HIGHER SELF** Students of **BROTHERHOOD MASTERSHIP.** He is a Lecturer and a Professor of this school. So from now on, if you believe and read "**THE FATHER'S TALK (GOD PRESENT)**" with **UNDERSTANDING,** you also become a tutor. The tutor is to introduce students to the school and lead them for Lectures.

When King Solomon **ETE** Lectures, not King Solomon **ETE**, but via **MY use** of His mouth, you can learn many things. **I** envelop Him and put Him on with **MY** possessing Spirit soul so **I AM** His soul and that means that **THE FATHER GOD** in Him is everything, because He is the way to **THE FATHER GOD'S** Lecture Revelations "**THE FATHER'S TALK (GOD PRESENT)**". This is because He has that boom as a computer inside of him. Therefore, dispatching this message to you means that when you acquire this **UNDERSTANDING** and this **WISDOM** for some time, you become a tutor, because you will not teach a new ones, you will not lecture something new. You only carry these materials that **I** give to go and lecture people. That is the meaning of being a tutor. Do you **UNDERSTAND**? *'Yes FATHER,' - answers Queen Disem S.D.* **ETE**.

As a matter of fact, anybody that acquires these Lecture Revelations and reads, could term them tutorial materials. That is saying you can acquire the materials and read or study at home like taking a home study course for students or in any other positive manner. **THE FATHER'S TALK (GOD PRESENT)** Lecture Revelations are the tuition materials. Therefore, you are now a tutor for the School of **HIGHER SELF, BROTHERHOOD MASTERSHIP.**

You *Queen Disem* have the right to introduce students. The students that will be introduced into **HIGHER SELF SCHOOL** will not be by chance. **I** will arrange it. All arranged people who are born naturally with arranged minds are the ones that can accept this arrangement. Other people will not **UNDERSTAND**. They will call it mystic and a secret society. They do not know that there is nothing that is mystical without spiritual secret revelations, but this is a positive secret of life.

THE SEERS – THE SEVEN FALLEN ANGELS

The secret cults opened by all the old masters where they hide and keep a lot of understanding for their personal consumption and initiate people secretly is termed a secret society. They have small, small keys that they know and can use to manipulate life. That is why they call themselves secret masters and they initiate people and charge them money. That is evil. They are organised through the fall away spirit souls. These spirits souls are seven angels that **I** sent to the world when they flaunted **MY** ordinance. They are named **SEERS** as the seven angels that **I** sent to control in-between the heaven and the earth. The **SEERS** prevent you from remembering what you know in spirit of your true nature when you come from any spiritual planet to the earth. When you come here, you become an ordinary human being so that you will not expose things, as you are not a **MASTER** to control yourself. On returning from the earth to the other side, they also stop you from remembering things. In effect, you do not take the **UNDERSTANDING** from here to there and from there to here. They have all those secrets in their hands.

These **SEERS** took assumed bodies, married and did all sorts of things and violated **MY** ordinance. Now, they stay there in-between good and evil till today. When you disturb **GOD** too much and **GOD** does not answer you, they rush to answer your prayer in a temporal way so that you would think it is **GOD** that answered has your prayer. Do you **UNDERSTAND?** *'Yes FATHER,' – answers Queen Disem.* They are not evil and they are not good because they are rebels. They behave as good spirits and practice soothsaying. They are the native doctors and elementary spirits souls who are telling people secrets of evil living and secrets of things. They established their children as their prophets and are establishing secret societies on earth in different ways and forms. They were the powers that **I** used to control the seven realms but they fell away. King Solomon David **ETE** is above that.

King Solomon David **ETE** is an open nation not a secret society. A society is a small place; even a country is a small place too. He is a whole nation, actually a whole continent like Africa, like Europe and like Asia. In fact, eventually **I** shall make him an open universe. **I THE FATHER GOD** in him is Secret and open Universe. What belongs to The **FATHER** belongs to the son. Oh, is King Solomon even interested in all these things! Don't you see how he *squats* (squats) in a corner like a baby? **I** told King Solomon sometime ago that if you don't behave as if you are around people will not see that you are around. You know the world is different now. He must put his feet down and behave as being around. Well, it is because of his nature, you know. His nature is like that, simple. Things of the sort do not really bother Him. However, if you follow His simplicity you do yourself a great harm. 'Oh Brother Solomon come and do that; come and do this' - that is what they used to say to Him. They did not know that they insulted **ME**. 'Oh, come and get this!' Anybody who has **UNDERSTANDING** should know how to treat a servant of **GOD**, because you don't know who is who. Do you see that the Lecture Revelation of this morning is very deep?

STAGE OF DEVELOPMENT DETERMINES YOUR BEHAVIOUR

Now you can see why people behave anyhow? There are those who call King Solomon **ETE** a secret society man and that He learned from Professor Assassu Inyang Ibom or that Assassu initiated him. The reason for their assumption is because they are stupid, not them, but their stage of evil life. They speak, as they don't know, but physically we do not call anybody stupid you know, because stupid means you have disgraced the nature. The stage of the person is not made by the person. It is made by **THE FATHER GOD**; therefore, if you really call somebody stupid it means that it is **THE FATHER GOD** that you have called because you are referring to **THE FATHER GOD**. Do you see how it is? If **THE FATHER GOD** has not upgraded the person, he would not know what he or she is doing. That is why somebody who has **MASTERSHIP** in Brotherhood cannot count sin for another person because he knows automatically that the person's stage is where **THE FATHER GOD'S** has put him or her. For that reason, if he or she counts sin and condemns the person, it means that he is insulting **GOD'S** authority.

Every mistake and behaviour of a person is naturally caused by the stage of that person. The behaviour depicts the level and extent of the growth of the person. If you reach a certain level and acquire the higher level of **UNDERSTANDING** then your behaviour will change. Children grow and change because they grow to **UNDERSTAND** life. Sometimes you do not have to tell them what to do. They start doing good things themselves because they've started to **UNDERSTAND** things. Whereas you used to talk and talk to hammer home some truths into them. When they don't **UNDERSTAND** beyond what they know, they think you are bullying them. Do you **UNDERSTAND?**

Is it only children who behave like that? Who else behaves like that, other than children? **I AM** asking you a question. *'It is carnal people'* – *answered Queen Disem.* Carnal people, yes, it is carnal people, but not really carnal people. It means the people who have not yet acquired the stage of **UNDERSTANDING.** They are not **MASTERS** to themselves. Being a spiritual person does not matter either. So many spiritual people still misbehave. They are spiritual, but they don't have **UNDERSTANDING** and they don't have **WISDOM**, so they are still at *'a, b, c kwakasikwak stage of life'* and that means that they are stupid. Is it not why, Our Lord Jesus the Christ said to Peter, 'get behind **ME**, stupid? That means Satan. Another name for stupid is Satan.

Anyone who makes mistakes and commits error is a Satan meaning stupid. The person is a Satan. Satan does not mean anything other than stupidity. That means a low mentality; you do the wrong thing instead of the correct thing. You speak bad words, instead of speaking good words. You are doing bad things, instead of doing good things. That is the meaning of being stupid as Satan or evil person. That was why Our Lord Jesus the Christ said, 'Father forgive them, because they are stupid, they don't know what they are doing.' It is lack of **UNDERSTANDING**, a low mentality.

So whether you are a carnal man or a spiritual man you need understanding to support whatsoever you are. In evil groups, they have understanding that is why they can practice proper evil in their way. All these secret societies gang up and use their evil understanding to kill people and to manipulate things in the world. They initiate people, train people and they practice evil very well. This is the same thing in the positive way, but the positive ways are very hard and those who practice goodness are very few. That is why **I AM** training people through this Lecture Revelation.

When **I** show people visions, they need to have **UNDERSTANDING** and **WISDOM,** to relay them well; otherwise, they'll talk rubbish. Suppose **I** show somebody something and he or she does not know how to present it, it may give a different impression. This is where you have to help as a tutor and as a physical lecturer. You have to help many people to become re-arranged brethren, and also help the people who are born a bit higher.

EACH GENERATION IS ONE CLASS OF STUDY

Small, small people in nature will not comprehend this Lecture Revelation and have this **UNDERSTANDING**. What **I** mean by small people is that naturally many people are born low. Those who come to this world, let's say, first, second, third, fourth, fifth and the sixth time still have problems, but those who come to the world up to seven times, oh wonderful, they are arranged human beings. Do you know why they arranged? It is because each time they come, they are in a class and you know that in the system of knowledge, each year is supposed to be one class of study. From there you progress to next class in the next year, starting from nursery. In spirit, it is each generation. Each generation, is each earth visit and you attain one thing but if not you move back to a lower class. Interaction in life means under going tests of life. It determines what you have learnt and how you **UNDERSTAND** it. How to love, how to give help to people, and how to speak well is all tested.

I TEST PEOPLE IN THE WAY THEY THINK, THE WAY THEY SPEAK AND THE WAY THAT THEY ARE DOING THINGS. THE WAY THEY MOVE, THE WAY THEY INTERACT WITH OTHER PEOPLE AND THE WAY THEY **LOVE**. **I** TEST PEOPLE IN **PATIENCE, MERCY, LOVE, PEACE**, ETC. ALL THESE THINGS GIVE MARKS WHICH ADD UP TO AN AVERAGE MARKS TO IMPROVED YOU.

When you have an average mark in all these subjects through your interaction with other human beings on earth then when you are transferred and come back, you start or improve from where you stopped. If you do not pass then you become lower. Some people have been coming and coming and they are still low. When you pass seven generations which are seven times on this earth and you are still low then **I** send you back to your original nature. If you were a tree, you come back to be a tree nothing more. Likewise, if you were an animal, a fish, or a bird in nature **I** return you back to that stage.

There are four living natures that **I** use after everything developed, to transfer the **HIGHER SELF** to a heavenly body to know **THE FATHER GOD**. The four living creatures are bird, fish, animal and man. So when the other creatures reach the stage of man they become a master to themselves. If you are still an animal or any of the other lower creatures you can invariably have knowledge and understanding, but you will be a master of this world. A master of the world can be a master of voodoo that is witchcraft. You can be a master of any secret society to kill people and to carry out wickedness on people. You can be the president to command an army to destroy people. You can be all those things. On the contrary, if you see **MY** own **MASTERS** come to this world, they are **PEACEFUL** and **LOVING**. They command **PEACE**; they command **GOOD LIFE, GOOD THINGS** and such have **MERCY, PATIENCE, HUMILITY, ZEAL** and the rest of the twelve powers. They will have any one or more of the twelve powers.

If you have a **MASTERS** or **DEGREE** in any of the twelve powers of man, of **ME, THE FATHER GOD, THE CREATOR OF THE UNIVERSE**, then you are okay. You become of one of the twelve tribes, the twelve calendar months of the year. So those who will work for **ME, THE FATHER GOD,** as the representatives of this kingdom will have at least, **LOVE, PATIENCE, MERCY,** and **PEACE**. They must have at least one of the **DEGREES,** which they will use to work in the Kingdom. This Lecture Revelation is part of your upgrade. It is for the student of **BROTHERHOOD MASTERSHIP, SCHOOL OF THE HIGHER SELF**. It is about being a **MASTER** whether in **KNOWLEDGE** or in **WISDOM** and the **SERVANT** in-between the two **CHAIRMEN**. Yes is **UNDERSTANDING**. That means that **THE FATHER GOD** has given you **UNDERSTANDING** now. **UNDERSTANDING** is not in only one thing, it is in everything. You know that when you are a **MASTER** and have **UNDERSTANDING** in all areas, you do not loose anything.

WHEN YOU ARE A MASTER

NOW BEFORE THE HAND TOUCHES, YOU KNOW WHAT YOU WANT TO TOUCH. BEFORE YOU TALK, YOU KNOW WHAT YOU WANT TO SAY. WHERE YOU ARE WALKING, YOU KNOW WHERE YOU ARE GOING. IT MEANS THAT WHEREVER YOU

GO, YOURSELF WILL BE HAPPY AND AGREE WITH THAT. Not when you've gone and come back, and then regret and ask yourself, why you should go to this or that place. Any time you go somewhere and come back to regret, that means you are not a **MASTER** of yourself. It means yourself is misleading you. Any time you say something and eventually you regret it, it means that you are not a **MASTER** of yourself. Anybody who knows what he or she says can never come back and regret and say 'why did I say that.'

With your eyes, you cannot go and look at something and say I don't know why I should look at that thing. If you do, it is because you are not a **MASTER** of yourself. But when you have the **MASTERSHIP,** whatever you see, whatever you say, whatever you touch, wherever you go and any other thing that a member of yourself is doing has been agreed and directed by the **CHAIRMAN** of yourself and you will never regret because they are all positive and good.

Before you talk to somebody, if you know that if you say it, it would offend that person, you would stop or find another way to present it. It is always **WISDOM UNDERSTANDING** and **KNOWLEDGE** that makes things work well.

Before you get up and say, 'in the name of our Lord of our Jesus Christ' and then begin to give a vision, you already know how to present the vision so that the person receiving the message will not break down. Where it is an unfavourable message or where the message is an admonition, you will not make the person to be annoyed. Even though it is a vision, your presentation will determine the recipient's behaviour. Even when you preach, there is a way that you may preach and everybody feels offended.

It is important that before you preach you should be sure that when you sermonize people will still remain happy. When you are preaching and pointing out, their faults and the words really touch them, then that should not cause them to be offended. Do you see that, all these things are very, very important in life - in the name of our Jesus Christ, in the blood of our Lord Jesus Christ, now and forever more, Amen.

HUMILITY IS IN THE HEART AND HUMBLENESS IS THE PRESENTATION

I keep King Solomon David **ETE** for the reason of making peace. If for instance when something happens around him and he gets confused for one second, he will kneel down and knock his head on the ground and ask **THE FATHER GOD, THE CREATOR OF THE UNIVERSE** to take control. That is humility.

Anytime something that is beyond your ability happens, even if it is not beyond your ability and you know that you cannot exist alone and that you cannot solve any problem, you knock your head on the ground for **THE FATHER GOD** that means that you are humble. Humility is not to appear humble physically by kneeling down while in your heart you are arrogant. Don't you see how people behave? Oh Brother Solomon, oh daddy, daddy as they are doing to the **KING OF KINGS** and would kneel down. As soon as they leave the place, they do what they want to do. Are they humble?

Humility is in the heart. When you are humble and have humility, it is in the heart. The humbleness is in the presentation of your physical self. You are humble before anybody when you present physically, but humility is in your spirit and that is in your heart, therefore humility and humbleness are working together to bring good fruit which is **UNDERSTANDING.** Humility and humbleness is one thing, one serves **PHYSICALLY** and the other serves **SPIRITUALLY**. The same thing with **WISDOM** and **KNOWLEDGE**, if they can have **UNDERSTANDING**, they will not clash. In the Lecture Revelation that we had the other day, it revealed that **WISDOM** always clashes against **KNOWLEDGE** because **KNOWLEDGE** is carnal. However, two of them can live for a better life. This life is lived by **WISDOM** and **KNOWLEDGE. WISDOM** and **KNOWLEDGE** built this house. So where will you live? **CARNAL** and **SPIRITUAL** have merged together to become one. That is what 'THE KINGDOM OF THIS WORLD HAS BECOME THE KINGDOM OF JEHOVAH GOD AND HIS CHRIST' means. That was **MY** plan regarding that revelation.

I do not want the Mother to control **KNOWLEDGE** anymore because she is doing it with arrogance and using it to fight against 'goodness which is **GOD**, so **I** have captured and invade it! **I** have invaded – O! That is why there is trouble. And she said that she will not give some of

MY children food because they stand with **ME.** She tortures them.

Take somebody like King Solomon David **ETE** in this world, who is suppose to be richer than Him? Is there anybody who would be richer than him? But the Mother does not agree. She says to him eh, you too love your Papa and your Papa loves you so much, go and eat **HIM**. Do you see that! She said 'okay let me see how he is going to survive, Jesus, Jesus every time. Now **I** bless King Solomon David Jesse **ETE**. What belongs to **THE FATHER** belongs to the Son, **AMFAR-ONE.**

Both **WISDOM** and **UNDERSTANDING** have to sign a memorandum of **UNDERSTANDING. I** have formed the shadow board. **I** use the shadow board now to maintain **PEACE**. You see! So to question is the first thing when misunderstanding shows its face using humility and humbleness.

MAKE A GOOD PRESENTATION

What is the spirit of misunderstanding in this Lecture Revelation?

"Not knowing something, yes, not knowing something that is lack of **KNOWLEDGE** on your own side. Not **KNOWING** something is misunderstanding, but it is called Satan, spirit of error and that is stupidity. You behave, as you do not know and present things falsely. What causes it? In this Lecture Revelation, what caused it? *"Lack of respect",*

So how did it lack? This is in your **KNOWLEDGE**. In **WISDOM,** what caused that are the low mentality and a low stage. It is not even mentality as such, but a low stage. The person is not growing in nature. He does not have Brotherhood **MASTERSHIP.** He or she is low. He or she does not have just a low mentality, but is actually low in his or her nature they are not grown up. For instance, people love **GOD**, but there is always something missing in the relationship. Somebody can love you, but if he does not **UNDERSTAND** you, he cannot make you happy. The love cannot be cordial. That is why it takes a long time for two people to come together physically and remain harmonious because of petty, petty things that create misunderstanding. This one will say, 'how can you behave like this' and the other one will also ask, 'how can you behave like that.' What will they take to conquer the whole situation?

UNDERSTANDING, Yes, **UNDERSTANDING**, What brings **UNDERSTANDING** easily?
'KNOWLEDGE'

No, it is **LOVE!!** How can it be **KNOWLEDGE? KNOWLEDGE** is of its own carnal state. **KNOWLEDGE** will never bring **UNDERSTANDING**. It is **LOVE**; it is **PATIENCE;** it is **HUMILITY** and **HUMBLENESS**. It is good **PRESENTATION; LOWLINESS OF HEART**. These are the things that bring **UNDERSTANDING**.

I just used Besemi to give an example regarding the way you asked her a question, yes? She may withhold from answering your question and it might not be arrogance. She could be shy or ashamed, but there is a way you could manipulate her and get what you want. You could say okay leave it for now, tell me some other time. When somebody is annoyed, he or she blocks all entrance. That is why **I** said **LOVE ONE ANOTHER** be **PATIENT**, be **MERCIFUL** and be **FORGIVING** among good fruitful characteristics.

All these positive powers help people to behave well and when you behave well, it becomes very easy to make a good presentation.

When people ask something of **ME,** they sometimes make their request with arrogance. They don't know that when they request something with arrogance they will not get what they have asked for.

Mastership and Understanding of Life

For instance, Our Lord Jesus the Christ narrated a story regarding the Publican and the Pharisee. Two of them went to the altar to pray. One said **FATHER**, 'help me I fast everyday, seven days a week. I am not like this man who has not fasted for even one day and he is a sinner. Truly, that man was a sinner and had never fasted. It is possible to know people who are physical sinners. The Pharisee was a holy man but because of arrogance in his presentation, he said it to the hearing of the sinner. So the sinner became ashamed and sobered. He shamefacedly said, 'Oh **GOD,** what my brother said is true. I cannot even fast. I am not good for anything and I can't even pray again. If you want to kill me, you can, but if you want, please save me and cleanse me.

GOD heard the prayer of the sinner more than the other one, because of what? **HUMILITY** in **PRESENTATION** that is **HIGHER SELF** King Solomon wants to live in a way that makes him appear stupid, but it is not because He is stupid, but because He is higher. Sometimes, higher **UNDERSTANDING** can make somebody look stupid in the face of **KNOWLEDGE,** but in the face of **HUMILITY** he is higher. Read: A Corinthians A: AG to the end.

A Corinthians A: AG – CA (1Corinthians 1: 17- 31)
>
> *"For Christ sent me not to baptize, but to preach the gospel: not with wisdom of words, lest the cross of*
> *Christ should be made of none effect.*
> *For the preaching of the cross is to them that perish*
> *foolishness; but unto us which are saved it is the power*
> *of God. For it is written, I will destroy the wisdom of the*
> *wise, and will bring to nothing the understanding of the*
> *prudent. Where is the wise? Where is the scribe? Where*

*is the disputer of this world? Has God not made foolish
the wisdom of this world?
For after that in the wisdom of God the world by
wisdom knew not God, it pleased God by the
foolishness of preaching to save them that believe.
For the Jews require a sign and the Greek seek after
wisdom: But we preach Christ crucified, unto the Jews a stumbling block, and unto the Greek foolishness;
But unto them which are called, both Jews and Greeks,
Christ the power of God, and the wisdom of God.
Because the foolishness of God is wiser than men;*
(You see that?) *and the weakness of God is stronger than
men.* (You see that?) *For ye see your calling, brethren,*

how that not many wise men after the flesh, (flesh – KNOWLEDGE) *not many mighty, not many noble are called:*

But God has chosen the foolish things of the world

to confound the wise; and God hath chosen the weak

things of the world to confound the things which are

mighty; And base things of the world, and things which

are not, to bring to nought things that are: that no flesh

Should glory in his presence. But of him are ye in Christ,

who of God is made unto us wisdom and righteousness and sanctification and redemption: That according as it is written,

he that glorieth, let him glory in the Lord."

'Peace in the name of our Lord Jesus Christ. Amen!'

You see that? The above Bible portion has answered so many questions regarding this Lecture Revelation.

UNDERSTANDING IS MIDDLEMAN TO WISDOM AND KNOWLEDGE however **KNOWLEDGE** must bow down to **WISDOM** because **WISDOM** is the **HIGHER SELF** of **KNOWLEDGE**.
Every carnal thing must bow down to spiritual things as the senior; because it is from spirit, the idea to create anything physically comes from.

All physical creations are second hand ideas because before you write, something down that thing must come from your heart. You think, therefore, the book cannot be bigger than the heart. However, the shadow cannot exist forever, because eventually what you thought of will go, but what you put down physically will remain. That is why **KNOWLEDGE** and

WISDOM must cooperate together to stop clashing. **UNDERSTANDING** is trying to bring them together to make a good of life. That is, carnal people and spiritual people must have love because spirit, spirit, spirit, won't you eat? Spirit, spirit, spirit, won't you need money? Spirit, spirit, spirit, will you not need to travel?

All the things that **KNOWLEDGE** brings are to help **WISDOM**, the spirit to survive, without which there is no way! On the same note, carnality or **KNOWLEDGE** should not boast over **WISDOM** because it will fail. That is why I said, "Where are the wise men of this world?" I thwart them because anybody that has **WISDOM** from above will bring down all the mighty people in this world put together. He will defeat them. A small child like a new born baby can defeat a big person if he or she is in spirit. That is why one should not joke with a senior person (a spirited child).

That bible quotation has covered a lot of things. **WISDOM** and **KNOWLEDGE** have to unit with **UNDERSTANDING.** Understanding is the middle power that has to help. From today, **THE FATHER GOD** has given you, *HRM Queen Disem Solomon David **ETE***, the power of **UNDERSTANDING,** and the power to have **MASTER** of **HIGHER SELF,** in the name of our Lord Jesus Christ, now and forever more! Amen!

Now is the time to thank **THE FATHER GOD** and praise **THE FATHER GOD** for this wonderful Revelation Lecture. Ikwo! (Song!)

HRM Queen Disem sings the following:
Song:

*"I am saying thank **YOU FATHER**, thank **YOU** my **GOD**. I am saying thank **YOU FATHER**, thank you my **GOD**.* (Repeat x-times)

Let **MY** peace and blessing with all the higher self students who read and **UNDERSTAND** this Lecture Revelation, Amen.

In the name of Our Lord Jesus Christ
In the Blood of Our Lord Jesus Christ
Now and forever more

THANK YOU FATHER

Mastership and Understanding of Life

Chapter Two

THE UNDERSTANDING OF LIFE
(RIGHT AND WRONG COMMUNICATIONS)

FATHER'S TALK
(GOD PRESENT)

Noah, Eleventh John, Father BOOE (AA.OG.BOOF)
(Tuesday Eleventh July, year two thousand and six (11.07.2006)

THE UNDERSTANDING OF LIFE
(RIGHT AND WRONG COMMUNICATIONS)

INTRODUCTION

Today, it pleases **THE FATHER GOD THE CREATOR OF THE UNIVERSE** to come down and dwell with man on earth. Christ said that **GOD** shall come down in person to teach man all things and bring everything to the awareness of man so that man will know himself and know all things brotherhood as well as know his **FATHER GOD**.

When a person knows himself or herself, then they know all things and everything becomes possible. When a baby is born on earth, he does not understand anything and because of that, the baby as a toddler and young child makes a series of mistakes and a series of errors. The same thing happens when someone does not reach the stage of

Understanding of Life. He/she makes a series of mistakes because of lack of understanding.

LECTURE REVELATION

As the **SUPER NATURAL TEACHER I,** bring this record out from **MY INNER-SELF** called 'Understanding of Life; Right and Wrong Communications'. The purpose of **MY** action is that **I** want all **MY** positive children of **THE FATHER GOD** to know who they are and know what they are doing so that they can live an arranged meaningful life on this earth.

When **I** said **I** will establish the Kingdom of GOD on earth and make this world become the Kingdom of Jehovah GOD and HIS Christ, it means that the people who will be living in this world, and manage it have to be of an arranged mind. Being that they are the likeness of **THE FATHER GOD,** not just image of **GOD** but also the likeness of **GOD**.

In the time past, all human creations were just the image of **GOD** because they did not have the likeness of **GOD** and as a result, there were killings, destructions, fighting and quarrelling. They were destroying each other because image does not know anything. Image is like your photograph.

Without your photograph, knowing it is a living soul it cannot help himself. The likeness is the light. Image versus image does not mean anything but when image is with likeness, then likeness will save the image in any pending problem. That is the reason that when you as a person see your photograph, you protect it.

If you see anything belonging to you, you protect that thing because you are the likeness of your image. That is what it is.

As you are the likeness of your image, you protect yourself against any destruction, because you know that under normal circumstances you cannot carry a knife to cut yourself or hurt yourself in any manner. You even protect your photograph and you admire it. You put your images in an album and preserve them. Anything that makes you admire yourself, you do it, because you like your image. Therefore, you protect your image and your physical self. That is the likeness of you that is doing that.

In like manner, if you are representing **GOD** in the likeness of **GOD**, you will love one another because everybody is you. They are the same image of you. They are part of you. You will not like to harm anybody because if you do, you harm yourself. That is the understanding. Love one another. Think well of other people; speak well about people and do well for people. Always use positive words because you know it is about yourself.

Therefore, the wisdom of today, which is 'THE **UNDERSTANDING OF LIFE,**' **'RIGHT AND WRONG COMMUNICATIONS'** has come as a wonderful Revelation Lecture to help those who are serious to study about meaningful and quality of positive life. It is for those who want to study how to become higher-selves and know **THE FATHER GOD**, and how to rule with **THE FATHER GOD,** and change the world to become everlasting new world, in the name of our Lord Jesus Christ.

PART ONE
SPIRITUAL COMMUNICATION

Key A: **PLANETARY ORIGIN**

Planetary origin is where your nature comes from. You know that nature is **THE FATHER GOD. I AM THE SUPREME NATURE** as **THE BUBBLE OF CREATION. I** use the original nature which is the planet that your soul comes from to develop you. Everybody that you see living in this world has to make life meaningful. This is the world where you live a physical life. Existence from every planet of the universe comes to this world as the centre to have a meaningful life and to progress their life's soul.

I have revealed this to you that this earth is the centre for education. It is a school ground and also market places where when you finish studying, you market what you have and improve, then you live a peaceful life. You can, from here go back to your planet of origin and come back here. You can carry out a meaningful trade here. This is where you engage in business activities. The meaningful business you do here is when you understand yourself and love one another, so that all will become well with you and your soul.

I AM THE FATHER GOD THE CREATOR OF THE UNIVERSE. I give **MY** Energy to all the planets including the soul planet, spirit, angels and man; living organisms and all living creatures to survive and to formulate a lot of things.

Communications that will provide improvement is positive pronouncements and positive utterances.

The origin of where you come from plays an important role to your life soul. If you come from the world of trees or world of fish or the world of animals or you are one of the terrestrial bodies from the star, the moon and all such planets, your souls of incarnations and generations are living there in transit. If you have your life connected to those worlds and you came down to this earth to meet the people here, you will still communicate with those in your planetary of origin many times without your knowledge.

In every original area where you come from there are families that you have left behind and that is who you are because you belong to them under that nature, but you come to this world as a trading ground. In this world, you meet with people whose origin you claim, because they are your physical father and mother.

However, it still remains that your soul of incarnation and generation is from the different planets you come from, which is your soul's origin. And that is why when you come here you have to pray to **GOD** and do what is good so that you can improve in understanding to be able to communicate back yourself with your real self.

If you have love and know **THE FATHER GOD** then **I THE FATHER GOD** will direct you. The problem is that a lot of people come here and do not know how to communicate back to their original self, because they do not know who they are and the result is that a lot of people link with others who mislead them. You cannot be a complete man or a complete positive human-god or human-animal if you do not know yourself or where you come from in nature. As you do not know yourself, you stand the risk of others swapping you with themselves and/or using you as a slave.

Mastership and Understanding of Life

When you do not have link from yourself that is, from your original self and know yourself, you will always be here as a slave. You will be doing what other people tell you to do and doing what other people are doing. You are not doing what yourself - the original you, is doing. As you are not doing what you should do, because you do not know, you are a slave to anything that is directing your actions because such directives may not come from the real you.

So the communication to your real self and your real planetary original father, which is **ME THE FATHER GOD** in different dimensions depending on the area you derive your energy from, must guide you to present the matter correctly. So that your assignment and what you came for on earth should be fulfilled.

Ninety-five percent of the whole world is living blindly. There are a few people who can talk and convince you to do what they are doing. Some people who are armed robbers may not be so in their origin. Many others join secret societies that harm and do wicked things to people. They may enter such things and do all sorts of horrible things for material gains. Such actions may not be in their origin because they do not come from that stock of that type of living.

It could be that you saw someone who is very rich and you wondered why you cannot be that rich. When you approached such a peerson and registered your interest to have his/her kind of money, he/she will ask, so you want to be as rich as I am? You answer in affirmation. 'Then I will show you how.' Will you follow me to do what I am doing?' He would ask you. You answer that you will. He then leads you to his/her means of acquiring his/her riches, which involves killing people and using them to get money and or also be involved in incantations as source of his/her wealth. Then you join him to do all those diabolical things which are not from your origin. In doing that, you are abusing your origin as the planet that you came from and you will suffer the consequences of you actions. As a consequence, you have failed in all your errands from your entourage as the power or authority that sent you - the Gods that sent you to this world to do one thing or the other for **THE FATHER GOD ALMIGHTY** for progress in life because if you progress here they will also progress there. They will come closer to that road. You are the link as the root for them to come through. As you have now failed yourself, you fail them and because of that, they cannot progress and so they punish you. That is what obtains. That is what happens in this world.

With every Planetary Origin, you must know and do the things that suit the area you come from so that they will back you up. **GOD** is the Spirit. **I THE FATHER GOD, AM ALL** and **ALL; THE BUBBLE** of **ALL THINGS; THE TOTAL IDEAS** of **BROTHERHOOD**.

Everything means **THE FATHER GOD** and **I THE FATHER GOD** now manifests **MYSELF** in so many dual forms just for positive coexistence of general life on earth and all other planets.

So whenever you see yourself at anywhere there is reason for it. Especially on this earth, there is a reason for you coming here as a human-being. The reason is never for you to kill; it is never for you to destroy. It is never for you to join any secret societies and practice wickedness or do evil in any way or form.

I, THE FATHER GOD, AM not negative and **I AM** not evil. Evil came from the enemy. It came from Satan, the bad one, the fall away energy of nature. So that fall away energy of nature is always around to mislead you into doing something that you should not do. It misleads you to communicate with evil instead of communicating with **ME THE FATHER GOD, THE ORIGINAL SELF.** With this inhibiting energy, the first key you need is understanding and awareness of yourself. If you have this, you will then pray and communicate with **THE FATHER GOD** to help you. You must ask for **THE FATHER GOD'S** help to do everything to have understanding and awareness that you are not an evil man and that you are not a negative person. You must confirm that you are from **GOD** and that you are positive. As a human being and as a human-God, you should love one another. You should think well and speak well of one another. Everything you do should be positive.

So when you understand the point of life described in Key A is your origin then you must do something to please your inner-self and to please all the other selves that sent you here on earth to be a way for them. A way to them is like being a helper to anybody.

For instance, a father in the family who is well established paves the way for all the children in the family to establish well too. That is the reason that in some families, if the father is a lawyer, the children or one of the children will follow their father's profession. So also for a father in the medical field, one of his children is likely to be a medical doctor too.

Whenever you establish on earth your children are bound to come down. Who are your children? Your children are the other Gods. They are the others of your planetary origin. They are your fellow selves that accompany you to pass through to come here into this world because everything is one.

So do good things. Think well, speak well and do well then everything becomes well with you, in the name of our Lord Jesus Christ. Amen.

Key B: **EVOLUTION AND TRANSIT OF BIRTH**

Coming to this world through your mother's womb is an evolution. It is another stage of life. You come on transit to this world through your mother's womb.

Evolution means progressing from a lower stage to a higher stage.

You cannot have evolution to the same level. It is either you move forward or backward. Evolution means change of a stage of life and then you go through transit periods. Transit is a temporary situation. It is a situation that is not permanent. From time to time when you get a point that is, when you take up the chance to take evolution, you grab that point and get higher in level.

It is only in this present manifestation world that you have the opportunity to help yourself to correct the past. If you know yourself, then you will know that what you should do is possible. You will then know that you should love and do good things to help one another. You will have the awareness not to involve yourself in negativism. When you have known all these things and perhaps in your last generations, you have made such mistakes then you must use this present time to now dissociate yourself from all those negative things.

When you have distanced yourself from all types of negative lives and evil practices in general, then you can now evolve to a higher consciousness of life. To achieve this higher life consciousness position, you must have love; be merciful and live peacefully with people. Armed with that understanding you now have the ability to practice these virtues of higher consciousness in your next transit into the world. Remember that your improved position is through having understanding to practice positive virtues that form the self in you, is the energy in you.

When you take birth into the physical world through a woman's womb and a father's seed, you will now practice your understanding of higher life physically on earth and help one another. That is when you become fruitful. However, if you do not understand that the life you have now is bad that is, you kill, you are wicked to people; you join gangs and bad associations to do ill to people and you do not understand such actions to be bad, then you cannot evolve higher. You will rather devolve to debase your soul. You will go back to become a demon as evil, willing other people to do more and more evil.

On the contrary, if you have the understanding that your present life is not good or the former life you lived was bad, you can take an evolution. The evolution in your present life takes effect when you say, '**GOD** give me the ability to love; give me the ability to practice peace and to make things good for people. Give me the ability to like people and do good things for people. That is the upgrade of your mind as the awareness of mind that forms evolution to your soul so that either here or there you will be able to change over to a higher stage of life. Your higher life will now bring good things for the generality of humankind and glorify **THE FATHER GOD** who created you.

That is the first evolution and transit of birth that you need to undergo. That is the reason there is a temporary death and temporary birth. Some people die and quickly come back to start a new life; because what they expected and what they came to meet differ.

For instance, the soul follows people. It may be that you looked at a family for one day and took birth into that family, only to discover that they are worshipping idols. Also, their activity or activities are not good and you regret that you were born there. Your regret is a demonstration that you have now taken a voluntary evolution. As you do not like the place, nature can transfer you. Death can occur to enable such transfer. You will then come back to the earth through another channel which will be a better ground to enable you to worship **GOD** or to do things that are better. All these things work through your pronouncements as your words.

It is what comes out from your mouth that is used by **GOD** to reorganise your future, because that word is **THE FATHER GOD.** So whatsoever you say registers. If you regret by saying – 'why should I be born in such a family; why should I keep company with this type of people; why should I do certain things that seem adverse to me and death is better compared to this kind of life because I don't like this kind of life.' If you say these words out, your regret is taking voluntary evolution, but you will not know that, that is what you are doing, that the **SUPREME NATURE** has taken note. Nature is **THE FATHER GOD. I AM THAT I AM** will now use your expression.

As **THE SUPREME NATURE, I** know your state of mind that you want to improve. The option is that temporary transit will take place and when you come back; your situation will be corrected. When you fail to realize that you have taken evolution then, you will go back to the same state. You will repeat such going and coming back for seven times. If at the end of your seventh return you do not have the awareness of your evolution, then final death will occur and that is evolution and transit of birth.

When you go through most of the Lecture Revelations in **THE FATHER'S TALK (GOD PRESENT)** from the King Solomon Spiritual Library, you will understand that to have the higher-self of understanding – the higher consciousness – the higher mind – the higher understanding, is the only way to progress and understand life. That is when your life becomes meaningful to you in your soul as a self-person and to another soul who is part of you and then **I THE FATHER GOD**, your original self will back you up.

Whenever you cannot have a meaningful life and understand how life is, then you are still in an elementary school. You need to die as many times and take many transits by force for evolution purposes to enable you to attain the higher-self. Without this procedure, you cannot progress in any way of life.

That is the reason that those who are physically here on earth and have in one way or the other finished their seven incarnations and seven generations are lucky. As you are lucky to come across this training, this **School of Higher-self,** it is imperative that you take on board this teaching because this is the final, final, final, closing, last, terminal, endmost, ultimate, finishing, concluding… final, final teaching.

We are now in the new generation. In this generation you need to progress because this is the last chance to do so. THIS IS THE GENERATION OF **'AFTER THOSE DAYS'** SAYS THE LORD MOST HIGH – THE VOICE OF **THE FATHER, THE POSITIVE VOICE OF THE FATHER GOD WITH SUPER UNDERSTANDING INTELLIGENT WORDS.**

With this, you will now understand exactly what to do and then use that to take evolution for your next life to gain access to the Tree of Life which is **THE FATHER GOD.**

Evolution helps you to pass from the Lower-self to the Higher-self. This is achieving by consciousness of actions; through emotions; by thinking WELL; by speaking WELL and by doing WELL, and doing good things then you will progress. If **I THE FATHER GOD** now sees that it is necessary for you to take physical birth, **I** will give you a short transit. You will take a new birth to correct the situation. That is where you cannot change your situation at your current birth place. As you cannot exercise that change physically, then **THE FATHER GOD** has no alternative than to implement spiritual transfer, which is that you have to die for a rebirth somewhere else. You should understand that in this situation you are not actually dead. You have only changed environment. Your picture could change and sometimes your carnal name might change, but your spiritual name remains the same.

That is key B, Evolution and Transit of Birth.

Key C: **MEETING POINT**

Where do you meet? The point that you meet matters because you have to speak well and think well so that you can re-arrange well. As you now understand that, your brother should be somebody who loves you. Your father is supposed to be somebody who knows **GOD**. Your mother should be somebody that has patience and a good character. When you know this, you have to speak well and take higher-self to arrange a meeting point by speaking well because a meeting point is very necessary.

Physically on this earth, you follow people you do not know to their homes, thereby risking exposing yourself to seeing rubbish. For illustration purpose – say you just met somebody, a man somewhere and the man professes instantly that he loves you so much but you do not know where this man came from, indeed you know nothing at all about him. You do not even know whether the man is a human being, but because he succeeded in convincing you, you accept his words. On your part because of the stage of life, you are as perhaps a prostitute or just desperate for a man because maybe you are lonely, you either take this man to your house or follow him to his. You might not know that this man is a ghost that lives in a burial ground.

At night, you follow this man to his house but how will you know this house is not a manipulated house. A spirit can flash your eye and you will follow him and see a beautiful upstairs building. You will not know that what you are actually looking at is a burial ground. It will be like a dream to you. He will take you and do whatever he wants and bring you back. All through you will not be aware that you are not in a living house, but a burial ground or it could be inside the water.

An animal can come out from the forest and take a human form to take a woman. You will then follow that animal back into the forest thinking that you are in a house. He will do everything for you, but he has spoilt your template. That is what the evil people are practicing. So without you knowing the origin of someone yet you follow the person, then you have gone to the wrong meeting point. Your action has resulted in you soiling your template and that means you have spoilt your life.

A virus has entered into your system in your life and it will take you ages to rid yourself of it.

Let say that an evil man died in wickedness and does not have access to reincarnate; it will go about as an evil ghost. These are the ghosts that evil people command and they go and work for them.

These people will now come and sleep with you and pour their negative blood into your system. Even just cuddling you and kissing you has the same effect. Do you not know that exposing yourself in that way allows for such communication to start in your physical life? You do not know because you do not want to know.

So when that action finishes and you go home, from that day your life cannot be the same again. Just as people always say – 'your life will never be the same again....' Do you know what they actually mean? It could be that they have infected you, with positivism or negativism and so your life will never be the same again. In relation to this part of this Lecture Revelation the wrong meeting point means that something foreign has infected you because of the wrong meeting point. That is the physical aspect.

The same thing happens when you are born into the wrong family or a wrong place. That is to say that you are a child of **GOD** who is born into a native doctor's home. And that means that you do not have the opportunity to pray to **GOD**, as they will use their native practices to prevent you from worshipping the real **GOD**. That means the meeting point is bad. Or you are a woman who comes from **GOD** and went to a man probably because he is rich. You get married to him and he puts the spirit of witchcraft into you and you become a witch then the meeting point is bad.

How many human fishes in nature are married to human fishes? How many human animals in nature are married to human animals? How many human birds in nature are married to human birds? And how many human **GOD'S** in nature are married to human **GOD'S**. It is always the case because you do not know. You follow beauty; you follow what you see. You do not know if this person has the same concept as you, and the same components.

If you meet a man and he has the same concept as you, there is the likelihood he may be from the same planet as you. If you see a woman and she believes what you believe, there is the tendency that both of you come from the same planetary area and are of the same nature.

If you think the same way speak the same way and do things in the same way and you have equal love for each other and Love for others, then in all probability, it is the right meeting. Contrast this with a woman who meets a man and sees that the man is wicked; he shows outright wickedness to fellow men and she still goes headlong and marries this man and she is a human-God female. Eventually it will dawn on you that this man in all truth is not a human-God and you will regret such encounter. He will also demonstrate wickedness on you and your children will also have this trait of wickedness. So tell **ME** how you can get out of this if you do not take time to check the point of meeting before committing yourself.

Let say, you have dabbled into the family of idol worshipping, and stored this meeting point in you then your next birth on earth will be within this family. Do you know the reason for this? You are a human-God that becomes involved with a family of idol worshippers or native doctor's family through marriage. As a human-God with the understanding that idol worshipping and diabolical practices of the native doctor are a no, no with **THE FATHER GOD** yet you still went ahead with such marriage, then when you die and are reborn on earth, you will be born there.

You have become a member of that family tree of idol worshippers. Consequently you are now included in that family rebirths of their area and type. So you better choose well! You better plan the meeting point well so that your continuation in continued siblings that you pass into the Tunnel of Souls around and around and comes back to your point should be meeting you well.

That is what Key C is about as The Meeting Point of Spiritual Communication.

Communication in this sense is what the nature uses to progress you or debase you. Nature uses communication as what you believe, what you understand and what you aim in your heart as well as what you wish somebody. They are all put together and used to refresh you or to recreate you or to evolutional you. Whatever it is you have for yourself as forward, backward, upwards or downwards of the progress of your life, is according to communication, registration and the meeting point. That is what happens as regards to this key.

Key D: **RIGHT MEETING**

Always think well. When you reach this Higher-self Training and your consciousness improves, and you become an arranged mind, then you will speak well. A lot of things have happened in your life which made you regret the type of life you lived. The mistakes you made in life, the sufferings and every other thing. Maybe it came from you or from the origin or the tribe, you incarnated from. So what you have to do now is to think well, speak well and do well to change that past and to change this present for a better future.

What you will say is that next time if **GOD OF NATURE** gives me the opportunity to become a human-God on this earth, I will have love; I will have peace; I will have patience and I will love everybody. No bad person will come to me. You should speak these entire things such as 'I will meet my other self. I myself in other half of myself will meet myself and arrange and live well together'. Do you see that you have to speak well? Of course, if you do not reach a certain level in nature, you cannot know exactly what to say. It is not very easy to talk good words, but easy to rap on and speak negative.

So if you speak arranged words because of the consciousness you have, what will come after will follow the events that are properly arranged. The nature will use the words to arrange things properly. What **I** mean by the Nature is **I THE FATHER GOD THE CREATOR OF THE UNIVERSE, WHO** is giving you the original insight of wisdom to meet well. Do not forget that **I AM EVERYWHERE, HERE** and **THERE**, so wherever you need **ME, I AM** there to improve your consciousness through this super wonderful Lecture Revelation.

The right meeting is to meet your real self. If you are positive, you should meet positive. Do not have dealings with people you know who have no positive conscience. You shall know them by their fruits. Even if the person is your mama or your papa, it does not matter. The person can be a preacher or Jesus or God, or anything so forget about names. Use ones fruits to know the right thing. Use your inner-self built psychology as a spiritual psychology to know the good thing.

If you bear good fruits, you will think well and you will speak well. What will come to you is well, well, well. From there you have the understanding to choose better things. So the right meeting is, always meet and associate with people who are positive for they will meet your standard. They will meet your understanding.

It will cause you a certain thing though because you lose something to gain something. Sometimes, before you have access to a positive situation or to have access to a good person, a lot of things will happen. I may not let you know what will happen but the situation will occur that before you gain any good thing you will pay for it somehow. Nothing is actually free. Satan will tempt you and try to change your mind from doing good things, which is the only price to pay and that is the steadfastness and faith in **GOD** with long patience.

If you see what you need, it may require some payment of sort, nonetheless getting it will be a good meeting and you will have a good future but if you run away maybe because of the apparent difficulty then you will never make it.

This boils down to the cross that is connected to **GOD** which means suffering. The little problems you will have like stress and so many things that will happen around you are for you to have a good and positive future. For that, you should not run away. If you do, you will not succeed then you have failed and you will not have a good meeting. So always, believe that you have to pay a price for anything good.

You should try to meet the same people that you know that have the same positive mind with you. Do not force yourself into people that you already know their behaviour to be questionable as the people that do not have fear of **GOD**; the people that they do not have love and the people that do not have peace. These people have no mercy for people. They talk anyhow, count sin on people and they assassinate people's character. Yet you still love these kinds of people; you associate and mingle with them. That means you have transferred yourself from the good side to the negative side, which is a wrong meeting.

If on the contrary you are having a good meeting point, which is the right point of meeting, you will change your evolution to suit that in future and your life will improve.

Key E: **WRONG MEETING**

The WRONG MEETING is the same as the right meeting but in the other way round. You have to make sure that your meeting is not wrong because if you follow wealth, beauty and the physical things, you will sure encounter the wrong meeting. For example, you want to be as rich as the other person is so you follow them to do what they are doing. That is what often happens therefore the meeting point will not be good.

For instance, you are from a Christian family that has the fear of **GOD** and you have in mind to marry a certain somebody. Your parents could even encourage you to marry someone because such person is rich and as a result, you marry someone who does not believe in **GOD**. You have chosen the wrong meeting point and then your offspring and your template will start to germinate from there. You have now totally lost it.

So if you are in spirit and understand, you will always ignore any meeting where there is no proper understanding. This always happens between a man and a woman as they establish themselves in marital obligations or when they start to have children. What type of meeting point did you have; what type of meeting are you having? Do you meet as human-Gods or as human-animals? Or do you meet as human-fish to human-fish? Or is your relationship that of human-animal to human-bird? What is the template of your the origin and offspring? Where did the person you meet come from?

They say oh, 'everybody in the world is together now. The world has changed.' The world has changed but changed to what? Did it change for good or to perpetrate negativism? What is the change in the world? You must ask yourself this question. You can see that the world changed and progressed in negativism. A lot of bad things sprang up everywhere in the world. However, that does not matter because this is the TIME OF PATIENCE. **I AM** using the patience of time to allow the change in people. **I AM** giving you time to change. For when **I** do away with negativism and you have not changed from your bad ways, you will have no point to be with **THE FATHER GOD. THE FATHER GOD** has nothing to do with anything bad. **I AM** not a negative **FATHER.**

This is the right time to choose the **CORRECT MEETING** and not the wrong one. Wrong meeting is when somebody lives in the water and goes to be with another on the land. Show **ME** the understanding that the water person and the land person will have. What type of meeting will there be where one comes from heaven and the other comes from the earth. How can the two of them become one, while there is a far distance in transit?

Demonstrate to **ME** what good meeting a bird and a fish have that is, between the water and the air. What good meeting can a human-being and a fish in the water have? All these things are the things you need to know. That is the reason that the School of Higher-self Brotherhood Mastership is paramount because through this learning and training you will be able to make the correct choice and book for the correct meeting. Though you have made the wrong choice now, later it can be corrected.

This is so far, the end of part one, **SPIRITUAL COMMUNICATION**. How you communicate and formulate the point of meeting, check the planetary origin, take evolution and transit of birth and arrange for a meeting point. Make the right meeting and not the wrong meeting. When you do all these things, you are now sure that your life 'understands life' and then you will live your life with the knowledge of the right and wrong communication.

PART TWO
MIXING RIGHT AND WRONG TEMPLATES

Key A: EVOLUTION OF NATURE AND IMPROVEMENT

Mixing the right and wrong template is what is going on earth and that is caused by the negative self which is Satan. The aim of Satan is to spoil the children of

GOD'S origin. He did it to Adam for instance.

When **I** created Adam, **I** knew that the earth is a point of the carnal world. It is not a spiritual world. So when **I** broke the egg of nature and saw that physical things are carnality **I** made sure that man will be having a spirit to help man grow. Then Lucifer being the negative part of **ME** came down and tricked man with the intention of mixing the wrong template that she has into man. This caused man to have a mixed mind.

She used snake to have the infusion of negative energy into Eve and Eve passed it to Adam. That caused humankind to have mixed templates. **I** revealed this in the 'Offspring.' **I** have revealed this in numerous Lecture Revelations of **THE FATHER'S TALK (GOD PRESENT)** that **I** have given. **I AM** touching on it again in this key A to help the situation, as it is very relevant.

This mixing of right and wrong templates is because of fornication and following people to do what you are not supposed to do. That is the reason fornication is very bad an act because fornication has something to do with the energy as the blood cell that relates to the creation of the environment of life.

After you have listened to all these, you know that anyone can bring infection to change someone's template. Examine the following illustration. You have pure water in a bowl as real pure clear water and someone of a dubious mind who is out to mete out wickedness to you drops a red or black liquid into your pure clear water. That contaminates your pure water and then it is no longer pure. Just one drop as a tiny drop is enough for the contamination to take place. Or the water is poured into a dirty container therefore, it pollutes the water and the water cannot be termed pure any more.

The next thing to do is to solve the problem and that is this key A as

EVOLUTION OF NATURE AND IMPROVEMENT. You have to believe that physically while you are here, you can change that. You can do this through listening to this study and following it, one after another, pray and communicate with **THE FATHER GOD** and become positive and **LOVE ONE ANOTHER**.

First of all, you struggle and practice to have five stars as indestructible five stars which are Mercy, Love, Righteousness, Kindness and Peace. They signify **THE FATHER GOD** as **Brotherhood** physically on earth. When you possess these five stars, that is you have love; you have mercy and peace and are peaceful and kind then you will be righteous which will help all these things that will help you take evolution to improve your live from the bad stage of misunderstanding to the right stage of 'UNDERSTANDING SELF'. This is the evolution of nature and improvement.

You have to come out from the stage you are. You need to improve because that stage is a natural one saddled with heavy sand. It is a heavy human being and it is blood and water. Now through the Spirit of our Lord Jesus Christ and the Holy Spirit of **THE FATHER GOD**, you can take evolution to improve your nature and rid yourself of the bad template.

This is because you were not originally created to be an evil person. Your circumstance is that you mingled with the evil ones and they taught you how to be wicked. From the time you know that evil is bad and you change, you have taken evolution to improve to positive life.

Key B: **WRONG CONTACT ADDRESS**

Assuming you take evolution of a new life from your previously negative existence. And say you were into armed robbery, you spoke evil, were a prostitute, a killer and you were really evil and did all sorts of bad things but you have now taken evolution to improve your life. You have started **PRACTICING LOVE FOR ONE ANOTHER** then someone comes along and calls you names that no longer suit you. You do not have to respond to that because the person is addressing you wrongly.

When you are addressed wrongly, it is not you they are talking to, therefore, you should not concern yourself about that because the contact address is wrong. The inside of you now is love, peace, mercy and joy. You think well of people and you represent **THE FATHER GOD.** For this reason if someone is, calling you all sorts of bad names such as juju saying that you are this and that, there is no need for you to panic about it because the person is addressing you wrongly.

However, the other side of it is that if you call yourself Jesus, Jehovah, the loving one advertising yourself that you are very good, you preach the word of **GOD** and do healings and all that but inside you are a wicked person then the CONTACT ADDRESS IS WRONG. You have talisman, you are a member of a secret society, you drink blood and you do all sorts of incantation then the contact is wrong. How people perceive you physically is not what you are in spirit or in the soul. Within you, you know that you are a wrong person and they address you as 'oh man of **GOD**', yet you accept such accolade knowing 'you are wrong'. The person coming to you is dealing with one who is wrong because are you are wrong. You portray one thing but represent something else inside you.

ADDRESS IS THE NAME OF A PERSON. A CONTACT ADDRESS IS THE FRUIT THAT YOU BEAR WHICH DIRECTS SOMEBODY TO YOU. Someone who wants peace must come closer to someone who is peaceful. If you have peace that is, a component of **THE FATHER GOD** in you called peace, those who need peace will have contact with you. They will communicate with you. When they start talking to you, they'll start to have peace. When they live next to you, they will copy the manner of peace. In all transactions, people will gain a peaceful atmosphere because peace is living inside you.

You are therefore the ADDRESS OF PEACE. You may not be called peace physically but because you bear the fruit of peace, you are peace. The same thing is applicable with all the twelve characteristics of the Holy Spirit, which are mercy, love, humility, life, faith… and all the rest of the good virtues.

If you have any of the characteristics of the Holy Spirit in you as a component of **GOD**, then it positions you to represent **GOD**. As a matter of fact, it makes you **GOD** because of you have higher-self. Consequently, you are automatically the address and the contact of that component of **GOD**. Anybody that comes to you will gain. 'I went to see **THE FATHER GOD**' is the appropriate reference that people should use because you have become **GOD PRESENT** as **THE FATHER GOD, FATHER'S PRESENT** because love is inside you.

They are unlikely to see love because love is a spirit and they cannot see it physically however they can see the house of love which is you as where love is living. As it is, the only way people will see love is through the house of love. When they say I'm seeking love then that will be you. You may not be called love but could be referred to as *OWO Etteh* or you could answer any other name. However, when they come to see you what will communicate with them is the love in you.

Okay some need faith and you are practising faith. You are a faithful person. You have faith in **GOD** as implicit faith in **THE FATHER GOD** therefore; **THE FATHER GOD'S** component called faith is residing in you as **MY** resident. You become the house of faith as Peter then when those who are seeking faith call you or Peter, they will have faith. When they come to Peter, they'll have faith. Though your name may not be Peter but spiritually your name has become Peter or faith. You have become a rock. You have become a key holder who holds other things for people. This is the reason people will come to you, because you are the harbour of **GOD**.

The components of **THE FATHER GOD,** which are the characteristics of the Holy Spirit are the Spirits called Gods. If they worship this spirit in you, invariably they worship you and worship **GOD**. Nevertheless, you are not the Almighty **GOD** because the **ALMIGHTY GOD** as **THE FATHER GOD** of all these spirits and all components is **THE WHOLE**. However, the component that you bear as the fruit is part of that worshipped as God but not as **THE FATHER GOD.** And is for this reason you will know that the contact address is not wrong. It is the right contact.

Whenever someone wants any of **THE FATHER GOD'S** components, like life and they came to you as the house of life then automatically you will give life to them. That is the correct address and the correct contact called **GOD PRESENT**.

GOD is the general term for the good character spirit of **THE FATHER GOD** dwelling in a place or in a man. And when you have any of these good components then you become the house of **GOD** called the Church of **GOD**. A church is not a physical place you sometimes go to call the Bethel or a place to worship **GOD**. These places are buildings put up by man for meeting together as a congregation. **However, human beings can meet in you**. This is a very deep revelation.

The whole world can come and meet in you. Assuming you are peace or you are love. You have **THE FATHER GOD'S** Spirit of love in you - **THE FATHER GOD'S** Spirit of peace in you; **THE FATHER GOD'S** Spirit of power in you; **THE FATHER GOD'S** Spirit of life in you; **THE FATHER GOD'S** Spirit of wealth in you then people can meet in you. You have **THE FATHER GOD'S** Spirit of all the amount of things from **THE FATHER GOD** then depending on how much you can acquire straight from **ME** as the **SUPREME CENTRE**, you become **GOD PRESENT**.

THE FATHER GOD is the Supreme Centre of everything. The more you are closer to **ME**, the more you believe in **ME** the more you work for **ME;** the more you become one with **ME THE FATHER GOD** because all these things become part of you. This will induce the whole world to come to you as God Present. Wherever you reside –wherever you live as a human being they can find life in you. In you, they can find peace; in you, they can find power; in you, they can find faith; in you, they can find everything good and that will attract them to you. Whether they like it or not they will come to you.

They will not come to you as a human being. They come to the house of God, the church and the temple. They will come to you as the Treasurer of God where they can get what they want. For all the people who do not have love, peace, life and any of the others of **THE FATHER GOD'S** components, will find that in you. If you are needy, you an orphan, you are destitute and looking to progress and find solace, you find it in the house of **GOD**. People are poor and in dire need of these virtues of **GOD** hence, they desperately seek them. And the only place they can come to get any of these is from you.

If people come to you, you will have an open mind to accept them. Just as **THE FATHER GOD** is free and has an open mind for everyone. Whomever that comes to you even if it is the whole world, as many as are looking for these components of **GOD** will find these virtues in you. Because, in order to get 'it', gain and then benefit from it, they must surely come to you. They have no choice.

Coming to you is that they come to worship **GOD** in you and around you because wherever you are, you are a child of **GOD**.

It is written that whomever that practices, **MY** word **MY FATHER GOD** and **I** will come and live that person and **I** will reveal **MYSELF** them. Wherever any of these components of God are practised, even if it is only one of the virtues, it will attract the whole world-the ones who are looking for such virtues to come to you. However, they will see you physically as you but in spirit, you are **GOD**. That is the reason people make mistakes.

When you see anybody that has just one component of **THE FATHER GOD**, living in him/her, do not joke with such person. You cannot kill him or her. If you try any rubbish, you will only harm yourself, seriously. This is not a matter of saying who is talking and who is not talking. This is absolute truth.

MY components are buried in man because man is **MY** city; man is **MY** country; man is the home and man is everything. That was the reason **I** created man. **I** created man so that all these components of **ME** will reside in man. When **I** say, **MY** child is love; **MY** son is patience; **MY** daughter is mercy that means all these daughters and sons are spiritual food of **THE FATHER GOD.** And they are **GOD**.

If you attract all these components to live in you and you bear them as fruits, you become the contact point of **ME.** You become **GOD PRESENT** and AMFAR-ONE Brosisco. You and **I** become incorporated in Christ. You turn into an anointed one of **ME.** You become an earmark centre, the ultra Modern Flashing Light that every soul must come to. Anyone that comes nearer to you will obtain salvation because they will see what they are looking for. Show **ME** who on earth or spirit or angel that can fight such a centre. **I** give maximum security and insurance to any such centre of man.

Who has a treasure and does not secure it? You will do everything to secure your treasure, including your treasurer. For if, someone has access to your treasurer that means the person can get at your treasure. That is how **I** give maximum protection to secure the House of **GOD** and the Church of **GOD**. And that is He whom **MY** components manifest in as God Present and that is that and what **I** mean by Contact Address.

If you go contrary to these things and encounter the wrong contact address then it means you will not see any of these components of **GOD**. You will rather see Satan or evil. You may meet someone as a beautiful person or a tall handsome young man but the person is a witch or a wizard therefore, what will you get from that person? There will be no peace and you are sure to have problems and get ill everyday. That is your wrong contact address. Wrong means evil and something that is not correct so you cannot find anything good there.

A person can be called love and another termed mercy however, they do not practice love and show no mercy then that is the wrong contact address. Another could be called Peter but has no faith therefore any little thing that happens he rushes to see a doctor. For a minor incident due to lack of patience, he takes someone to the law court. All sorts of wrong advice will ensue from such people which are very misleading, because the person you contact does not represent **GOD**. He or she represents Satan as evil therefore if someone calls you Satan and you practice evil, you are appropriately addressed.

If you see negative spirit, negative practices, incantations, acts of wickedness as evil in someone then the person is Satan because what lives in that person Satan therefore he or she is the address of Satan. Satan is feasting with that person.

On the other hand, when you see goodness, love, peace or any small goodness in a person, that individual is the address of **THE FATHER GOD.** You can call that person **GOD** because he or she is God Present.

That is exactly what it is regarding the wrong or Right Contact Address.

Key C: **MISSING THE POINT**

How are you missing the point? You are missing the point because as you do not have spiritual awareness, you have no understanding, then you are missing the point. You are missing the point because like a lot of people something, has blinded your eyes. Carnal things like beauty and handsomeness blind people's eyes.

You are not looking for spiritual things that will help you. If you are rather looking at and considering carnal things then you are missing the point. The longer you miss the point, the longer it will take you to correct yourself. And whatsoever happens to you, you cannot blame **THE FATHER GOD.**

Is it not what happens to people? You so like to grab things you see in the world. You want to be rich overnight. You want to be all sorts of things and because of that, you involve yourself in a lot unsuitable things. As you are carnally trying to help yourself, you miss the point.

All these things are communication. You use your mind to search for it. You should communicate well with **THE FATHER GOD** and speak well of people and wish well to others and so on. All these things will guide you because they will line up for you. And from there you progress because whatsoever you sow that is what you will reap.

If you do not want to miss the point, all you have to do is struggle in all the possible ways to get the five stars. Attain **mercy** in your heart; **love** in your heart; **kindness** in your heart; **peace** in your heart and obtain **righteousness** to know **THE FATHER GOD** and to love **THE FATHER GOD** in your heart.

When you have these positive five stars that can never be destroyed because they are indestructible, then you have the correct point. You are then not missing the point. Where you do not have any of these things, you are missing the point, indeed you are joking. You can sing-o! Shout-o! Call Jesus! Do whatever - sleep in the temple –o! Do whatever you like; you will still be missing the point.

This is exactly what obtains in 'Missing the Point.'

Key D: **WRONG CHOICE**

To make a wrong choice is actually to miss the point. If you make a wrong choice, it is because something has blinded your eyes. It shows that you do not believe there is a better future, so you make a choice based on carnality.

So many people make wrong choices for their children. Even on making, their own choices a lot of people go wrong because of the aspects they take into consideration. They choose carnally, thereby resulting in the wrong choice.

I THE FATHER GOD is here on earth addressing these issues. A good person who is interested in making the right choice can do so on reading or listening to one of **THE FATHER'S TALK** or listening or reading **THE EVERLASTING GOSPEL** or imbibing the **SPIRIT OF BROTHERHOOD,** which is truth. That name alone Brotherhood means one family of the same parents. That name alone will not allow anyone to think evil about someone else. Missing the points and mixing things stems from making the wrong choice by ignoring the positive side of **GOD**. When you go and choose the wrong side **MY SOUL** always hates that!

Why do you kill? Why do you involve in killing someone so as to become rich? Why do you engage in assassinating people's character so that you can earn a position? Why do you do things for material gain, which is temporary when your conscience tells you it is wrong? For what you gain through unrighteous acts and falsehood will never last. That is blatant exhibition of really making the wrong choice.

So think well; speak well and do well and then **THE FATHER GOD** will open your eyes to make a good choice for yourself.

A good choice must be directed by love, by patience and by the Holy Spirit. A good choice must be when you are truthful to your heart and your conscience. A good choice is when you do not stand with negative and talk bad about positive. If you stand with negativism against positivism, you will never conquer. So the wrong choice is the worst mistake anybody can make. That is the mistake that when you make, it costs you a lot to correct.

Now that this type of Revelation Lecture has come out from **THE**

Mastership and Understanding of Life

FATHER GOD, you have to make sure that the choices you make are correct. The choice of husband, the choice of a wife; the choice of work and the choice of life in general because every choice you make connects to life. Do not make a choice that looks good today but tomorrow; it affects your template, your physical life and spiritual life. Avoid the choice that will land you into everlasting doom; a choice that you see **THE FATHER GOD** yet you muck about and don't want to know.

I know that a lot of people know the truth. They know that Brotherhood of the Cross and Star, is the Kingdom of God on earth. However, due to not getting the nature of their quest in physical life, they deny **THE FATHER GOD.** Everybody knows that **I, THE FATHER THE CREATOR OF THE UNIVERSE, I AM** capable to do anything but **I** do not force the situation. If **I** force you to do something and it is not from your mind, then eventually you will change back to what you are. You may even do more evil than your previous one.

So, when you accept **THE FATHER GOD** you accept a situation in your spirit that becomes interwoven as cemented inside you. It becomes the faith in you for you to know your situation is from **GOD**. It is just like a man who really, really loves a woman. No matter how ugly or bad in character that woman is or how marred, he will use his love for her to contain and forgive her.

Similarly, a child who respects his or her papa has no choice regarding who, what or how he is. As soon as you know that, this is your father, whether he is short or tall you accept him. You have no choice there. On the contrary, something you can choose requires carefulness so that a bad choice will not boomerang on your intended good will.

Key E: **FRUSTRATION**

Frustration comes through the wrong choice. When you make a wrong choice, you become frustrated in your heart when events take place. You look for wealth by all means so you approach a juju-man, who asks for your child as a sacrifice. You agree and enter into a contract, thereafter you pray to **GOD** not to allow such a thing to happen. You have already dabbled into it for your prayer to be effective. You made the wrong choice and now you are frustrated. Satan runs away, deserting you. So why don't you have patience.

You marry someone because this person is materially rich. One in the marriage you discover that this person is using their money to control you. You now shout because you are frustrated. A wrong choice always manifests frustration in ones life.

You made a wrong choice by not worshipping **THE FATHER GOD** in your youth. When you grow old, you have no back-up with **ME, THE FATHER GOD** rather you have back-up with evil. People give excuses for not knowing **GOD**. They will say it is because I went to school; oh it is because of this and that, I do not know **GOD**.

You do not even want to help anybody; and you do not do anything about **GOD**. You do not worship **I THE FATHER GOD THE CREATOR OF THE UNIVERSE**. You do not even know **HIM** but you want to live a meaningful life. You are making a wrong choice. When something happens and you go looking for **GOD**, by that time **GOD** is no more interested in you because what you sow is what you reap. If you work for **GOD**, **GOD** will work for you.

I THE FATHER GOD with **MY** love and mercy is revealing these things so that you will start to make a good choice. Cement your heart with the choice you make so that whatsoever happens you know it is your choice and you will then not frustrate yourself.

However, if you have never, ever, ever made a good choice and stand well as a positive person in the positive heart then your frustration is worse.

The point is that many families force their children to marry the wrong persons and they frustrate their children's lives. Many parents force their sons to marry the wrong women causing frustration for both. Likewise, daughters are coerced into unsuitable marriages. A lot of people force themselves to do things against their will. They go where they are not supposed to go and meet with frustration. Then they lament. What caused the lamentation? It is quite obvious. They made a wrong choice and met with frustration in their lives or in their soul. Frustration in the physical life, frustration in the soul and frustration in spirit is the worst thing that can happen to someone. Frustration in your spirit is caused by frustration in your soul. Frustration in your soul is caused by frustration in your body as the physical life.

What you do here does not stop here. Some people opine that what you do here finishes here. No! It is not so. Everything you do in the physical life affects your soul. If it is good, it makes your soul happy because your soul is your storage called the storeroom. Soul means the place you store things that you will later get back. Whether you like it or not you must get back what you stored in your soul. It is automatic.

Without an object, there is no shadow. So long as you are an object, you must have a shadow and that shadow represents you. In that similitude, your soul is you. Anything you do as the choices you make and what you practice is retained in your soul. Your soul can then frustrate your spirit when you do something that contravenes what is in the spirit. In other words, your action is not originally registered in your spirit. Maybe as a matter of 'can't help situation' you did what you shouldn't and got frustrated in the three capacities as the physical, soul and spirit and that is when you become sad. Why should people become sad? They did what they should not and worried about it afterwards. What comes after is sadness and eventually frustration follows.

However, if you are okay that is, you made the right choice and you are with the higher-self which is **THE FATHER GOD** then nobody, no soul and no spirit can frustrate your life. Nothing can get you frustrated because **I THE FATHER GOD AM** around you.

When **I** gave a Lecture Revelation about **MY** creation of human beings, **I** made you know that **I** did not create everybody individually. **I** only created Adam and Eve. Actually, **I** did not create Eve until later. **I** created Adam first and eventually created Eve. So the two (Adam and Eve) multiplied into the physical world till tomorrow. Subsequently you stand the chance to be either negative or positive.

When you make the good choice and worship **THE FATHER GOD** in spirit and in truth and practice love for one another and forgive one another, you will assuredly live a peaceful and reasonable life. Continuously, leave everything for **THE FATHER GOD** and frustration can never come anywhere near you for **THE FATHER GOD** will not allow it. You are protected in all the entirety of your life, in spirit, soul and physical. You will not have any frustration because you will not frustrate anybody.

If however, you made the bad choice and mete out wickedness to people by sometimes disguising yourself and cause the downfall of someone, then it will happen to you. You will be frustrated because that is what you sow.

As in the good choice, if you do good things and are truthful to people then, your way of life is good. You have improved in life then nature which is, **I THE FATHER GOD** as **THE SUPREME NATURE** will use that to upgrade your life.

Key F: **MAKE WRONG COMMITMENT**

Frustration will cause you to make wrong commitment. When you frustrate your soul then your subsequent actions frustrate your physical life. All three are constantly frustrated as your physical self, your soul and your spirit. Being thus frustrated you become down and enter into bad commitment, which will of course result in trouble. From there you start floundering about looking for help and assistance and that is likely to induce you to make the wrong commitment.

How do you make the wrong commitment? You go to a visionary because you have this problem. The visionary says to you that you should go and throw things into the river; buy chicken, eggs; buy this and that and a mirror and throw all of them in the river for *mami-water*. When you do this, you have committed yourself wrongly and you have become a wanted person. Your conscience starts to blame you and that is a wrong commitment.

That is the reason the Bible said, if you want to save your life you lose it, but if you leave your life for **GOD, I** will save you. Why not then leave everything for **GOD** when you have a problem, instead of following bad advice that gains you nothing only for you to make the wrong commitment.

You will say - oh I love this person too much but that person is a juju man. If you proclaim to love someone too much, you will prove your love by involving in that person's type of life totally.

A situation occurs that a man loves a woman so much. The woman capitalizing on that will say to him – I cannot follow your pattern of life you have to adapt to mine. In your heart, you know she's living wrongly but you have no choice than to enter into that wrong commitment. You know you are very much averse to the things she does but because of your deep love for her, you commit yourself wrongly by accepting to follow her. Your action now frustrates your inner-self. From then onwards you encounter all sorts of problems.

How many people are in this world that do not frustrate themselves and others? How many are there who do not know what they are? People of this world tend to talk well because they believe what they say. How many of them can come out openly to speak about positive things without fear? They cannot because they are all committed - wrongly. They are all in the wrong commitments – the whole lot of them but they pretend that all is well.

Therefore, if you want to avoid the inherent destructive effect of wrong commitments as well as others in that line of living, make a good choice. Correct yourself before it is too late and allow

THE FATHER GOD take stress and frustration away from you.

Leave everything for **THE FATHER GOD** in patience, in love and believe in **ME THE FATHER GOD THE CREATOR OF THE UNIVERSE.** Have faith in **GOD** and forgive one another and start to yield the good side of **GOD** in you. When you start to see happiness and joy in your heart, then your stress and frustration have been wiped away.

Key G: **THE CONFUSION STAGE**

Whenever you get involved in the wrong commitment, you are gradually falling apart and going down, down and down. You are on the downward escalator.

From the meeting point, you made the wrong choice. And from the wrong choice, you met with frustration. From frustration, you start to do what you should not do. You commit yourself where you should not; you keep the wrong or bad company and do what you should not be doing. You are going into the confusion stage of life. You can no more understand what is happening to you.

Oh, my life has fallen apart, I don't know what happened – you moan. It is confusion. You no longer know yourself. Why is it so? It is because you left **THE FATHER GOD** and **THE FATHER GOD** allowed you to your ways.

When **I THE FATHER GOD** leaves you and throws, you to all these types of situations then you become wrong. What you should know is that nobody can do anything good by himself or herself except through **THE FATHER GOD.** It is that communication part of GOD that will lead you to do what is good and that stabilizes your situation. The contrary approach brings frustration and from there you have a confusion state of life. Confusion state of life is very bad. Some people kill themselves. Some others reason that they are already bad and might as well continue with their negative ways of life.

I THE FATHER GOD nevertheless, through this Lecture Revelation and teaching has devised this simple means for you to go through and correct your situation.

When you listen or go through to the next keys, endeavour to imbibe and implement the necessary actions to the latter, which addresses the way you can retrace your steps through your dark life excesses that led to your confusion state.

Key H: THE CAUSE THE EFFECT AND THE MATTER

You have to retrieve yourself from your present predicament. Ask yourself what caused this kind of confusion to me. You will come with the answer that it is mixing the right and wrong templates as a grave mistake you have made in your life.

You ignored **THE FATHER GOD** which is your positive self. You ignored all the advice **I** give. When somebody approaches such matter, you affirm that there is no **GOD**. You insist on living a fast life; you strive on living as a carnal person and that spells the cause of your misfortune in spirit, soul and physical.

Think about your life for tomorrow. Think about how to improve it. When you know that, your predicament is not from Satan or juju or any such things but from your choice then change your choice. It is from you – yourself. When you realize that you are a sinner and have done bad things to people and you do not have love, you do not have mercy; you are not God Present then change and have the components of **GOD** in you so that you can become God Present. From the moment, the realization hit you that the cause(s) of your frustrated and confused life stems from you through the choices you have made then you have started thinking well and you will have the opportunity to think about a remedy.

You will now start to worry about the remedy. You worry about how to overcome this temptation in this stage of life as a life that has no meaning; a life that

Mastership and Understanding of Life

is not good; a life that does not bring joy to you; a life that with all your stupendous financial and physical wealth, you are not remotely happy.

How can you be happy with that kind of life in the confusion stage as where you know that something is wrong but have no idea how to go about putting it right? The saddest thing is that when you die in that condition, you come back to face the music. The stage that led you to kill when you should not kill; a stage that led you to steal when you are not supposed to steal; a stage that led you to wrong commitment, to consult a soothsayer and do all sorts of things you should not do. Now you are looking for a remedy and that is when you have to come back to **THE FATHER GOD.**

You must come to acknowledge **THE FATHER GOD** as a **PHENOMENON THE ALMIGHTY GOD, THE CREATOR OF HEAVEN AND EARTH.** Then you will come to **ME** with the understanding that **I, THE FATHER GOD, THE CREATOR OF THE UNIVERSE** is the remedy. That is when you will have the solution to your problems.

PART THREE
THE REMEDY

Key A: **THE SCHOOL OF THE LOWER SELF PRIMARY; SEVEN TESTS OF BROTHERHOOD**

When you come back to **ME, THE FATHER GOD THE CREATOR OF THE UNIVERSE** with the knowledge that **I AM** the only **ONE** who can correct your mind, change your situation and template and engineer a new life for you, then Brotherhood comes into the matter.

The Key A of this stage is to be conversant with the time of Adam. You need to remember that **GOD THE FATHER** is **THE FATHER** of all creations. That everybody came from the same parents; everybody came from the same source which is **THE FATHER GOD** and that it is through love that **THE FATHER GOD** created everybody.

Coming to this stage with your penitent heart, **I THE FATHER GOD** will turn **MY** merciful eye on you and welcome you as a prodigal son or daughter into **MYSELF.** Thereafter, you will know that all the experiences you encountered from your planetary of origin to the present has been training. All the ups and down of your condition were training. Your eyes are now opened. And you will now look for **THE FATHER GOD** and look for a REMEDY. You want to get away from the stage you are. You want **THE FATHER GOD** to cure the cause of your situation. And you want to improve that low mentality of yours so that you become a good servant of **GOD**.

The first step is to address your person as a servant of **GOD**. Tell yourself that you are not worthy to be a child but only to serve GOD. When you humble yourself before **ME THE FATHER GOD, THE SUPREME SPIRIT OF NATURE** then **I THE FATHER GOD** will start coming to you. You would have passed all the temptations you came across one after the other.

The seven tests of Brotherhood stand for the seven generations. All the generations are for training and you need to go through them for such purpose. That is the reason **I** said that this earth is for training. It is the centre for training. It is a school ground. You will see more on this in the primary stage of brotherhood.

Our Lord Jesus Christ is the first Son of **THE FATHER GOD,** which is Adam. Adam was low in nature because of his creation with mud, sand and dust. Eventually **I** put Adam's soul into Abel and his (Adam) spirit into Christ. Then Christ came to die for man's sins and passed the brotherhood test of 'love one another.'

You past through seven generations and pass the seven tests and surrender yourself to the cross which means love. From the day, you start to practice love for one another; confess your sins and do not count sin for people then it shows that you have passed the stage of a low mentality to a higher consciousness of loving one another.

The five stars of **THE FATHER GOD** is mercy, love, righteousness, kindness and peace that signifies Brotherhood. When you acquire these five stars of Brotherhood, **I** will give you the certificate that elevates you from the seven tests of Brotherhood to Key B, **THE REMEDY**.

Key B: **THE SCHOOL OF EXPERIENCE, THE SECONDARY TEST OF BROTHERHOOD: FROM CROSS TO LOVE**

The School of Experience is that when you start to put the love into practice, you will come across all sorts of temptations.

People that you love will hate you. People you do good to will connive among themselves and give you a bad label. You are not to curse them. You should still love them.

Acquaint yourself with the life of our Lord Jesus Christ, who is the Father of all human races. HE came and died for man and the human race does not know that this is their Father. As it is written, HE came to HIS own but HIS own did not know HIM. The world was made by HIM but the world does not know HIM.

What did HE make the world with? It is the **SPOKEN WORD**. The potency of the Spoken Word materialized itself as Jesus the Christ to kill that carnal body to redeem man back to **THE FATHER GOD**.

How many people on earth voted for Christ with regards to all the healings, all the miracles and all other many things **HE** did? People still crucified **HIM** and still hated **HIM** because they did not know what they are doing. That was the reason

HE made that pronouncement: '**FATHER** forgive them for they do not know what they are doing and that is the School of Experience.

When you are going through such experiences, the very loving wife you married could hate you; the very beloved husband that married you could hate you. Your child could change and be hurling insults at you. The very mother that gave birth to you would want to kill you. As you may realise, all that is unfolding around you is the experience.

The test of Brotherhood in this capacity is to love in that you must take the cross of love. Love them; think well of them; speak well of them but be careful in your communications with them. When you love your enemy; pray well for them and the whole world and **THE FATHER GOD** sees that you love, **HE** will make you God Present. That is when you have conquered. That is Remedy B as School of Experience in Life. What you see everyday, the events that occur in your life, the cross that you carry, which are the sufferings and all sorts of things you pass through in the name of serving **GOD**. Why are you serving **GOD**? In reality, you do not see **GOD** to serve but you serve **GOD** through other human beings.

What a preacher tolerates from his or her members; what you endure from the family you are helping; friends who do all sorts of things to you as you are passing through this School of Experience is all in the service of **GOD**.

At this stage of Brotherhood from Cross to Love, you are heading to Key C. You will be promoted by **THE FATHER GOD** to Key C, which is The School of the Higher Self to acquire the stage of indestructible five stars.

Key C: **THE SCHOOL OF HIGHER SELF: TO ACQUIRE THE STAGE OF INDESTRUCTIBLE FIVE STARS**

Through your experiences, your average points scored will be marked under the categories of Mercy, Love, Righteousness, Kindness and Peace and that signifies the true Brotherhood. Now you are successful and have become a Brotherhood in yourself. The kingdom of God is established in you, which signifies the first stage of everything going well for you and everything becomes well. Your life now is pure because **GOD** is living inside you. You have now crossed from death to life, which is from cross to star by loving one another, being Higher-Self and having understanding from which you acquire the indestructible five stars.

This stage of life is a meaningful life. It is an understandable life. You now apply to be the servant of **GOD** because at this stage you can help anybody. **GOD** can use you to encourage others. And **GOD** can now use you to improve others. You now become the servant of **GOD** whom **THE FATHER GOD** will manifest through. That is what obtains in Part Three, Key C of this Lecture Revelation.

In this stage wherever you are, you are God Present. **GOD** now talks through you. Your eyes become **GOD' S** eyes; your ears become **GOD'S** ears including all the rest of you. The five components viz. mercy, love, righteousness, kindness and peace will be leading you to acquire six and seven components and so on. Hence, you have become **THE FATHER GOD'S PRESENT** as God Present.

Remember that one component alone can help you; reason therefore what five can do for you. So now, you have remedied yourself and reunited with **THE FATHER GOD THE CREATOR OF THE UNIVERSE.**

PART FOUR
UNDERSTANDING OF LIFE

It is at this point that you now **understand life** which is the actual meaning of this Lecture Revelation. At this stage, you now understand life and you exclaim *wow oh*! So this is life! Your eyes are now open. You now see people coming to you for help because of the component(s) of **THE FATHER GOD** in you. Along with that, you will not puff-up or raise your shoulder because you know that you do not exist. You are not love; you are not mercy; you are not patience; you are not kindness however, kindness, love, peace and mercy live in you or and many more components.

THE FATHER GOD is all these components therefore; it is the component of **MY SPIRIT** which you bear as a fruit that lives in you that makes you to be God. That is the reason the name of **THE FATHER GOD** is not God. The title of **THE FATHER GOD** is not God. **I AM THE FATHER GOD. HE IS THE FATHER OF ALL GODS AND POSITIVE SELVES.** The POSITIVE SELVES are the **FRUITS OF GODS** which is **THE HOLY SPIRIT.**

THE HOLY SPIRIT is the Divine part of **THE FATHER** while the Male part of **THE FATHER HIMSELF** is ALL and ALL. Recapitulating, the Divine part of **THE FATHER GOD** is called The Holy Spirit. It is not the Mother Earth. She is quite different from the Divine part of **THE FATHER GOD** which is **THE HOLY SPIRIT. THE HOLY SPIRIT IS THE TRINITY IN CAPACITY. AND THAT IS THE COMFORTER.**

With this **UNDERSTANDING OF LIFE,** you now start to acquire these components of **THE FATHER GOD**

Key A: **HIGHER CONSCIOUSNESS OF LIFE AND SELF AWARENESS**

This is the stage that you become a leader as the representative of **THE FATHER GOD.** As a Christ's Representative and a Christ Servant, anybody that reaches this stage is God Present. You are in **THE FATHER GOD** and **THE FATHER GOD** is in you because you can now understand **THE FATHER GOD** and **THE FATHER GOD** understand you too. You become one and the same partner. You are no more different from **THE FATHER GOD** and **HE** is not different from you. **THE FATHER** is now relaxed with you. Your feet is changed and your legs too; your eyes are changed and indeed the majority parts of your body changes to that of **THE FATHER GOD**. For this reason, the **Higher Consciousness of Life** is the stage you are now living as well as into and further pursuing and that is the beginning of **the understanding of life**.

In this stage of **Higher Consciousness of Life and Self Awareness,** you now know what you should know. With this awareness, the reality dawns on you and so now you say, 'oh I actually do not exist.' There is **A PERSONALITY** out there! There is **SOMEONE** involved in creation. There is **SOMEONE** involved in making the whole world to be what it is. There's

SOMEBODY, A BEING involved in the creation of animals, the creation of fishes, birds and human beings and indeed in the creation of the whole world and the universe. So I should ADORE that **PERSONALITY** and that **PHENOMENON.** I SHOULD ADORE **HIM.** I SHOULD WORSHIP **HIM.** I SHOULD KNOW **HIM.** I SHOULD SERVE **HIM** because I came from that **PHENOMENON.** And who is that?

It is **THE FATHER GOD THE CREATOR OF THE UNIVERSE**

You now have the understanding that **THE FATHER GOD** created you in **HIS** own likeness and at this stage; you are the likeness of **GOD**, not only image. Image is just the resemblance but likeness is a particular thing as the self of that thing; the replica of that thing. Image is just a picture but you are not only a picture, you are the inside of that thing. You are the same thing.

In **HIGHER CONSCIOUSNESS,** you cannot hate because if you do, it means you hate yourself. Whatsoever, you do, you do as **GOD'S** Representative but you are not claiming **GOD'S** glory. You are using the blessing to improve and take more evolution to the higher situation and be exposed to a further consciousness of **GOD**. At this juncture, you start to really know yourself which is Key B of part four.

Key B: **MAN KNOW THYSELF AND YE SHALL PASS ALL TESTS**

When you are here, you will pass every temptation that comes to you because **THE FATHER GOD** will pass all of them for you. Temptation might not even come; Satan has no need to tempt you because it will be a waste of his time. It certainly becomes a waste of time for Satan to trouble you or anything harmful to come your way. Nobody can kill you; nobody can harm you. You are as free as the air because you and **THE FATHER GOD** are one. **THE FATHER GOD** is in you and you in **THE FATHER GOD**.

Your word is **GOD'S WORD**. Your leg is **GOD'S** leg. Everything about you is of **GOD**. Man knows thyself you have passed all the tests of Brotherhood. That is what it is.

This stage is The House of **GOD**. Whoever has seen you has seen **THE FATHER GOD.** You are humble because you know **THE FATHER GOD** is HUMILITY. You love because you know that **THE FATHER GOD** is LOVE. You have power because you know **THE FATHER GOD** is the POWER.

The power you have is not to kill but to reconstruct; to bless and to change things. However, anybody that brings death to you will die automatically because it is not you that will kill the person. The kill will kill, kill. Evil will kill evil. It has nothing to do with you because at this stage you have passed all that nonsense. Your feet are lifted off the ground. You are now in the higher stage of **GOD'S** consciousness.

Key C: **THE RIGHT COMMUNICATION**

The right communication comes in automatically at present status. This time **GOD** talks through you. You do not have words again. You no longer have a say and you have no idea of yourself. You do not even have a home, as your home is the home of God and the church of God. This time, **GOD** totally operates through you because you do not operate any more. You no longer exist. You are now the destination to **THE FATHER GOD** and **THE FATHER GOD** is to you.

So the right communication will change things for good. You will now speak as **GOD** speaks; you now pray as **THE FATHER GOD** prays. Everything is as **FATHER'S TALK, (GOD PRESENT)** because at this point the situation has corrected itself. When the situation has improved itself, you will now believe that **THE FATHER GOD** has taken control. And when **THE FATHER GOD** takes control, you have no problems again in any situation. Every situation that corrects itself is a demonstration that **THE FATHER GOD** has opened the way and you will know that you are now in the correct place.

The right communication means talking with **GOD** and **GOD** talking with you. Talking with **GOD** and **GOD** talking with you means that rather than having issues with somebody, **THE FATHER GOD** solves the problem for you. Where you could hate someone **THE FATHER GOD** changes him or her for good because you have the right communication.

The right communication is, when somebody thinks evil about you, they will confess by themselves. This is an automatic operation! And that is **I** in **THE FATHER GOD** and **THE FATHER GOD** in me. What you are saying are not from you. It is **I, THE FATHER GOD** that is saying those things through you.

You walk **I THE FATHER GOD** walk.
You look **I THE FATHER GOD** looks.
You hear **I THE FATHER GOD** hear.

When your name is called, **THE FATHER GOD** comes out and answers and so it becomes the right communication. Whosoever that talks to you cannot have bad dreams in their sleep. Rather **GOD** blesses them because they have communicated directly with **THE FATHER GOD.** You have become the Church of **GOD**.

You will now know how to correct the future. Your life becomes the future. You can now correct the present and from the present, you correct the past for the future.

Key D: **THE RIGHT CHOICE**

You can now have the right choice because **THE FATHER GOD** knows what to choose for you. You are no more the one that makes the choice and therefore will not choose wrongly. If you have to make any choice about a partner,

THE FATHER GOD in you will know that **HE** also created a woman the day **HE** created you and **I** will link you with that choice. **THE FATHER GOD** knows that you are a human-animal and **I** will link you with a human-animal. If you are a human-god, **I** will link you with a human-god. **I** will choose everything for you because you are in the centre of **UNDERSTANDING LIFE**. You no more live your life according to what you detect. Life itself detects for you because **I AM THE FATHER GOD** and you are a Master.

    As **THE FATHER** lives in you, **I** will make you a Master. Nothing you do is done as a primary student but as a degree holder, a master's degree or a PhD degree holder. So now, **GOD** is making the right choice for you. Regarding the right look – you look for what **THE FATHER GOD** wants you to look. You see what **THE FATHER GOD** wants you to see. You touch what **THE FATHER GOD** wants you to touch and you go where **THE**

FATHER GOD wants you to go. You will eat what **THE FATHER GOD** wants you to eat. Everything you do is what **THE FATHER GOD** wants you to do. You are now impregnated with **THE FATHER GOD** and you will give birth to **THE FATHER GOD** and you have no choice for yourself. You incorporate **THE FATHER GOD** into yourself and **THE FATHER** incorporates you into **HIMSELF.** So you and **THE FATHER GOD** are **ONE**.

Therefore, every choice that comes into your life is the choice of **GOD** and it must be right because **GOD** never makes a wrong choice. **THE FATHER GOD** will make the choice that will improve your generation; the choice that will make you rule with **GOD** forever; the choice that will make whoever comes closer to you to have comfort because they are with the right person. Even Satan will be comfortable and happy because he knows you are good. Satan loves good things. All evil people know good things, it is only that they cannot be good themselves. In truth, they know what is good and like what is good.

So therefore, that is the Key D, part four as The Right Choice. It will come automatically from **THE FATHER GOD** who directly possesses you and that means that in that direction, you and **THE FATHER GOD** are **ONE**.

Key E: **CORRECTION OF ERROR**

As **THE FATHER GOD** has made the right choice for you, the error is corrected. For all the many generations that you came and did not marry the right person, **I, THE FATHER GOD** will put right the correct woman for you and vice versa.

You lamented, oh why should I involve myself in these things? It is because you did not know what you were doing. How many people in this world marry the wife that was created for them? Have you not heard what Solomon said? 'Blessed is the one who finds his wife.' How many people in the world find their actual wife?

When you do not find the sibling of yourself, the wife of your heart, things always go wrong. The children will be wrong and everything goes wrong. When you meet the right person, you think alike and do the same things then what comes out from you will be Semsem (same-same).

Do you not see that any time you make mistakes; it shows that the left and the right cannot be the same and cannot lead to the same destination? The left leads to a different way and the right goes to the opposite direction. Therefore, this is what is happening. Correction of error occurs when you have made the right choice. When you make the right decision, the error is corrected automatically. When you make the wrong decision, the error persists.

So for you to feature in the Kingdom of God, to represent and to rule with **GOD** in the New Paradise of **GOD** on Earth you have to make the correct choice. And who will make this choice for you? It is your Higher-Self which is **GOD**.

The error of your past corrects automatically from the day you make the correct choice.

For all **MY** children who have been failing in other generations and have had one problem after another, **I** do not count sin for them. That was the reason **I** came as our Lord Jesus Christ in Adam to die so as to forgive humankind his sins because **I** know that events that man encounter in this world is for training.

However, this time around man should **understand life**. When humankind understands life, he starts to live life. Those with **understanding** are the people that will live a meaningful life on earth without killing each other; without destroying each other; without any conflict and no segregation. The right channel will be set for you to meet your aim and objectives of **THE FATHER GOD**.

When you put the screw into the right hole, it will fit in tightly but when you put the screw in the wrong hole, it will not hold. I put everything in twos with their correct pair. So why can you not find yours? As you did not attach **THE FATHER GOD** to your decisions, you have made the wrong choice and error comes in but error in what? -Error in thinking; error in speaking and error in doing things. When you think wrongly, you must surely speak wrongly. And when you speak wrongly, you must surely do wrong. Equally, when you think well, you will speak well and when you speak well you will invariably do well.

Key F: **THE NEXT MEETING AT THE RIGHT ADDRESS**

Now, being that everything is correct that is, the meeting now is in the correct address so who is the addressee? It is your name and this must be correct. And the in-dweller in that address is **THE FATHER**

GOD. So whenever you go to someone who is in the correct address, you will see the person. Unlike going to a place and they will say to you sorry it is the wrong address. Or you are told it is the wrong number and the person you are looking for is not there. Or that the person does not live there anymore. For when you live at an address that is not permanent, you always pack out to some other place. Packing out is confusion. You lose some chances and a lot of good things. So you see, it is not a good life to be packing out up and down.

Conversely, when **GOD** lives permanently in you every time, everybody would see that you are at the correct contact address. The right address is the next meeting that you are meeting. Your wife will always meet you and you will always meet your wife. Your children will always meet you because what comes out from you will always come to you.

As a man if you speak well, those words become children and will always come through you. If you meet well, then that meeting will always bring the mother of your children and she will become your cabinet and your record.

When you read the Lecture Revelation titled, ***CABINET, FILE AND RECORD***, you will know about a man, a woman and the children. You will know that they always go around and come around because everything is correct.

Key G: **FINDING YOUR OTHER HALF**

Through this, you will know that when you were born, **THE FATHER GOD** created you in two, a man and a woman. When you as a man was created, a woman was also created at that particular time as a half of you to make you complete. So every man that does not find the other half of him should know that his other half is out there somewhere. That is what is causing confusion up and down.

I indeed wonder how many people are really able to find their other half. The law of marriage cannot work when you do not meet your complete self. Whomever you meet as a man is your sister. Every woman is your sister. However, some women were men in their former nature. Not only that but they could come from fish or animal as sub human of that while you are a human being. So how can that work?

If **I** create a human-fish, human-animal or human-bird, **I** also create the same half, as a woman human-fish or woman human-animal or woman human-bird. This is so that when they meet, they will be compatible and problem free being the same template and created for one another. But mixtures are causing all sorts of confusions all over the world. Which family can you come across that does not have an evil person? This is due to the nature of marriage, the blood and the mixing of templates.

The sin of the Father Adam continued to generate all over the world and spoil things. Where is peace? Where is love? The only love people know is by saying – 'oh the world has become one now.' They inter-marry and thus profess one world. Soft Skin man (White man) marries a Thick Solid Skin woman (Black woman) or vice-versa and they all live together. Despite that, have you seen peace? Until the understanding of love and life becomes attached to that oneness, it cannot work but when that happens the world becomes wonderful!

There is no real corporation in the world; people only corporate to practice evil ignoring **THE FATHER GOD THE CREATOR OF THE UNIVERSE.** People corporate among themselves to spoil the world but they do not come together to correct the world.

So what we are talking about is oneness with **GOD** to do correction and to form the new world that will be peaceful and a paradise on earth.

So finding your other-half is not possible for a mere man. It is only possible with **THE FATHER GOD** when everything is corrected. It is from that point of remedy that when there is **understanding** in the Spirit-soul then Nature will link you back to your other half. When both of you find yourselves and meet then that is the end of the problem. Afterwards what will come out from you both will be Semsem, the same you all the time.

Key H: **CORPORATION WITH YOUR OTHER SELVES – YOUR SOULS OBJECT OF CREATION**

This point is that after you have found your other half who is your sister or brother, your wife or husband (as you call here on earth) what will now be incorporated to start coming from your stock will be yourselves which has been multiplying.

If you have a child now, that child is both of you. The child will be the same as you with the same **understanding**; the same love and the same peace. So there will be no problem in that family and that is the city of GOD; that is the kingdom of GOD and the nation of GOD because you do not hate, so none of your child will hate each other. You do not kill so none of your children will kill each other. You do not indulge in incantation or believe in juju or witchcraft. You do not have any evil spirit, so none of your children will have it because your other selves, the many positive selves that multiplied have come in incorporation with you through **THE FATHER GOD.** They will therefore come through you and be born here on earth to take evolution to improve.

This evolution they are taking is to improve their lives to a higher consciousness because you are there as a teacher for them. A good father and a good mother are good teachers for their children.

All births will improve. Even your former spirit that incarnates through you will improve and you will also improve. From there everybody eventually becomes one and that is the progression of the **understanding life** that **I AM** talking about.

Having reached this stage everything becomes well- so far so good. We have now come into the conclusion.

PART FIVE CONCLUSION
MEANINGFUL LIFE

Key A: **MEANINGFUL OF LIFE**

At this stage, the life that you live will become meaningful to one another because you are now living a life of oneness; a life of peace; a life of hosanna and hallelujah; the life that nobody will ask what brought this person here; a life that you live and you can be a President, a King or a Queen. You are a leader of the community because your life becomes life of everybody. You are infusing good things to everybody that sees you because you are representing **GOD**. You represent **THE FATHER GOD** just as your children represent you and become everything to you.

Therefore this is the Kingdom of **GOD** that **I AM** talking about which has started to surface to manifest the understanding of life in the Kingdom of God.

Key B: **IDENTIFICATION WITH THE ORIGINAL SIBLING**

This time, the original siblings identify themselves through you because of the correct stock. Unlike the mixtures that prevails currently. Whatsoever that comes close to and comes out from you will be to your attestation that it comes out from you because it will show the sign. Love will give birth to love. Peace will bear peace and you will become a family of Peace, a family of Love; a family of Mercy; a family of Faith, a rich family and every good thing will come from there because it is coming through good siblings.

The lives will be similar to pineapples. Pineapples continuously bear fruits and when you cut one to eat, another fruit ripens and is ready to be eaten. All the time there will be fruits available. There won't be any lack at all. Siblings upon siblings will continue to manifest - original siblings with no mixtures. There will be identification spirits to show the fruits. Through the fruits, you will know the original siblings. You will know by the fruit that a sibling is the original from **THE FATHER GOD** that **I** have brought back to manifest **MY** glory in that place.

Key C: **EITHER HUMAN-GOD OR HUMAN-ANIMAL**

Siblings of human-God or human animal will continue to generate or come out from the stock and they will be revealed through identification whether it is Abel or Cain. If it is Abel as the offspring of positivism, the lover of **GOD** and the child of **GOD**, then you will know because the Holy Spirit as the identification soul of Abel will continue to identify his children. There is no way you will not know.

Then the negative spirit will also identify the negative spirits of animals that were already on earth, which interrupted the original plan. They formed themselves out to be human beings through the interruption that occurred between snake and Eve and later involved Adam. This presented the opportunity for animals to take evolution to become human beings hence the human-animals on earth.

When Eve was not deceived by serpent which is Satan, there was no tendency for anything like human-animal. **I** never put human-animal into creation because **I** never created human-animal. **I** created Human-Gods. **I** said **I** created man in **MY** own image and likeness which was Adam and later Eve.

However, the oxymoron spirit, the disagreement spirit, which is the carnal and negative self, the earth, wanted to rule the earth with carnality. So it infused that instinct into Eve and Eve passed it to Adam as Eve passed it to Adam when Eve became pregnant, Satan had the choice to bring animals physically on earth as humans, which is Cain. Cain represents Serpent as the original serpent, the father of the children of vipers.

Abel represents Adam, a Human-God. And that is why there exist these two forms of human beings on earth, which resulted four living creatures' altogether developed and manifested into human beings. Through the serpent, the nature manifested three of these creations, which are the human-animals, human-birds and human-fish however; the human-gods are the pure creations of **GOD**. All the three living creations came through Adam, so also the multiplication of the real man.

The real man developed from Abel while the other three developed from Cain. That is the reason there are confusions all over the world, but thanks to **THE FATHER GOD,** who sent **HIS** only begotten Son our Lord Jesus Christ to come and die on the Calvary tree to pave the way for **THE HOLY SPIRIT OF TRUTH** to come to the earth to teach man, all things are well. Now **I** come as **THE COMFORTER** to bring the awareness of human being and all the teachings and understanding back to humankind and sanctify humanity once more.

Therefore, if your mind is correct and you reach this stage of higher consciousness, then you will know yourself and become one with **GOD** again and then the original sibling will now materialize. For now, it is the mixtures abound that are deceiving people. Nevertheless, there is going to be extractions of positivisms that will stand by themselves that will know themselves o with **THE FATHER GOD.** The separated negativisms will also stand by themselves. And all belong to **THE FATHER GOD** therefore, love will reign for eternity.

Key D: **IMAGE AND LIKENESS OF GOD'S NATURE**

The Image and Likeness of **GOD'S** Nature is what **I** have revealed. I have given the explanation in depth in that the image is the carnal man and the likeness is the spiritual man. You see **I, THE FATHER GOD THE CREATOR OF THE UNIVERSE** has these two spirit selves as image and likeness; knowledge and wisdom, then understanding serves as the secretary. Understanding is like the Holy Spirit, **THE DIVINE CONSIDERATION OF THE FATHER GOD.** It is sort of neutral. It assists in all developments and provides help all the time to lead things well.

A **WOMAN** represents understanding for the **MAN** as the *secretary*, while **MAN** represents *knowledge* for **THE FATHER GOD** as the vice Chairman and **THE FATHER GOD** is the *wisdom* the chairman, the last authority. When the three work together, everything becomes well.

This is not happening because today in the world Scientists say there is no **FATHER GOD THE CREATOR OF THE UNIVERSE,** that there is only science and as a result they have failed woefully. Nonetheless, today, **I** have brought **MY WISDOM** back as **MY OWN SELF** and **UNDERSTANDING AS THE HOLY SPIRIT** and then built into the image of man who represents **GOD** as **KNOWLEDGE and** combined becomes The Trinity **GOD.** Because of this arrangement, *Knowledge*, the *Wisdom* of **GOD** and *Understanding* will make life easy. That is the reason this **SPIRITUAL UNDERSTANDING OF LIFE** is established on earth today.

From today that **I AM** revealing these things, **I** spray this capacity of awareness of **UNDERSTANDING** to all **MY** positive children and they will see that **MY** IMAGE has been revealed; **MY** LIKENESS has been revealed and the good news of the nature of the children of **GOD** has been established on earth. They are without sin; without death; without sickness; without problems; without killing; without war and without the ill-treatment of a fellow human being.

Now all the countries of this world and their governments will be made of children **GOD** as human-Gods that will rule and not the human-animals. All the human-animals, human-fish and human-birds who have repented and are positive and have the five stars will be serving the Human-Gods and become God's image all over the world.

Key E: **ABILITY TO SAVE OTHER SOULS (HELPER AND THE SERVANT OF THE HOLY SPIRIT)**

This is the spiritual power **I** give as the spirit soul energy of Servantship to all **MY** positives Servants as the new world leaders. At this stage, **THE FATHER GOD** will relax because they will rule with **THE KING OF KINGS AND THE LORD OF LORDS** in this world. There will be no problems again because those who have this certificate of *MASTERSHIP* with *UNDERSTANDING OF LIFE* will know how to serve the people and keep them happy. They will give water free; electricity will be free and all other necessary amenities as accommodation and good roads will be free. They will make life easy for everybody. Whatever **THE FATHER GOD** gives you, you will share it equally to all brethren because that is the Kingdom of God. And that is the "*PERFECT UNIVERSAL BROTHERHOOD*" that will materialize physically on this earth, which **I AM** starting from April next year (two thousand and seven upwards).

I declared in the budget that everything on earth belongs to **THE FATHER GOD** because **I** own them all. And every creation must acknowledge **THE FATHER GOD**. If you do not we will wear or put our legs in same pair of trouser and **I** mean it.

Key F: **AMFAR-ONE BROSISCO**

When **I** give you, the ability to serve souls as a helper and the servant of the Holy Spirit then that means the Holy Spirit is piloting you. **I** will use you at any point in time to save one another because you are God Present. For your eyes are **THE FATHER GOD'S** eyes; your voice is **THE FATHER GOD'S** voice and so on. You are the instrument of glory as the instrument of **GOD**. That is the meaning of being a leader; that is the meaning of being Kings and Queens in the Kingdom of God. You are the servant of **THE FATHER GOD**. That is the reason **I** say all Kings and Queens are servants of

GOD. The world shall see goodness; they shall have peace; they shall see joy; and see many blessings.

With this, **I** will map the whole world and when **I** certify **MY** children who are God Present, **I** will keep them around the mapped areas and those places will become the Cities of Refuge. **I** will give them power to rule but in essence, they are not the ones ruling, it is **I THE FATHER GOD THE CREATOR OF THE UNIVERSE.** They will be the light of **GOD** shining all over the place for eternity and that is, **I and my FATHER are ONE – Brothers and Sisters Incorporated in Christ.**

Christ is the anointed Spirit as the Chosen One; he is the chosen Spirit that **I** use to amalgamate the world to be one as the oneness of God Present, **THE TRINITY FATHER.** And with this understanding, everybody is one and it is joy, joy, joy, joy, joy!

From today, all principalities and all things that do not bring glory to **ME THE FATHER GOD THE CREATOR OF THE UNIVERSE** will be put under **MY** feet! **MY** children are rejoicing all over the world. There is no death, no sickness, no problem and no misunderstanding of life. All things become one and well with all **MY** children! –And now we go on to Key G – **GOD PRESENT**.

Key G: **GOD PRESENT**

GOD PRESENT means that wherever you see any of **MY** children you see **ME**. Whenever you hear from them it means you are hearing from **ME** because **I** talk through them as **THE FATHER'S TALK (GOD PRESENT)** as **I AM** talking now through The Senior Christ Servant King Solomon David Jesse **ETE** of **Ete** Royal Universal Family, Brotherhood of the Cross and Star, Ikot Okwo City, Nigeria. **I THE FATHER GOD** talks similarly through other people whenever **I THE**

FATHER GOD wants to talk, as **I** used to talk through people in time past. However, this TALK that **I AM** TALKING now is a little different and better because **I AM** not talking via Angels.

Anybody who believes this word, and shares with this good faith and understanding is blessed and progressed through this Lecture Revelation. However, no one who shares a negative mind can hear the light of this life. When you read or listen to this Revelation Lecture, you will know that reading or listening to it will give you a REMEDY if you take it into yourself. And at the end of the day, it will make you to become a child of **GOD** because evolution takes you to the child of GOD status either now or then. You will then rule with **ME THE FATHER GOD THE CREATOR OF THE UNIVERSE** and that means that you are blessed for eternity, now and forever more. Amen

In the Name of Our Lord Jesus Christ

In the Blood of Our Lord Jesus Christ
Now and forever more

THANK YOU FATHER

THANK YOU FATHER.
THANK YOU FATHER.
GOD BLESSES HIS HOLY WORDS.

SO I HAVE SPOKEN! SO IT IS WRITTEN! SO IT SHALL BE DONE! IT SHALL COME TO PASS FOR ETERNITY, NOW AND FOREVER MORE. AMEN.

THANK YOU FATHER

PART FOUR

THE INSPIRATIONAL WRITER

KING SOLOMON SPIRITUAL LIBRARY
THE GOD ENCYCLOPAEDIA WORD OF INFINITY

INSPIRATIONAL WRITERS AND READERS OF THE
FATHER'S TALK
(GOD PRESENT)
KING SOLOMON SPIRITUAL LIBRARY

In the name of our Lord Jesus Christ, In the blood of our Lord Jesus Christ, Now and forever more, Amien

(A) REFERENCING THE FATHER'S TALK (GOD PRESENT) IN KING SOLOMON SPIRITUAL LIBRARY

I know that some people will be inspired when they visit King Solomon Spiritual Library website or bookshop, and have access to any of **THE FATHER'S TALK (GOD PRESENT)** information through books, electronics, audio and otherwise and are inspired to write or produce any information through the knowledge that they have gained, they must not fail to reference **THE FATHER'S TALK (GOD PRESENT)** in **King**

Solomon Spiritual Library as the source of your inspirations.

(B) THE WORD OF TRUTH AND THE HOLY SPIRIT PRINCIPLES

Since **THE FATHER'S TALK (GOD PRESENT)** is the direct information from **I THE FATHER GOD ALMIGHTY HIMSELF**, all positive children of **GOD** can be, and will be inspired with this **WORD** because the **WORD** of **THE FATHER GOD, THE CREATOR OF THE UNIVERSE** is a Spiritual Case Study for all souls to improve to have self awareness and a Higherself Consciousness.

When you are inspired and you want to write, make sure that your ideas, principles and concepts are based on the Holy Spirit of Truth without changing the ordinance of the **FATHER'S TALK (GOD PRESENT)**.

(C) THERE SHALL BE CONSEQUENCES THAT WOULD FOLLOW THOSE WHO USE THE MEANING, THE CONCEPTS AND THE PRINCIPLES OF THE FATHER'S TALK (GOD PRESENT) FOR THE PURPOSES OF MISLEADING

Consequences shall follow those who use the meaning, the concepts and the principles of **THE FATHER'S TALK (GOD**

PRESENT) for the purposes of misleading in any manner.

Any Human-God, human-animal, human-bird or human-fish who has access to **THE FATHER'S TALK (GOD PRESENT)** through any means, be it via books, electronics, audio and otherwise should know that those words are not the words of human beings. The words are transcribed, proofread and accepted by **ME THE FATHER GOD** as it comes from the **SUPREME STUDIO OF THE ALMIGHTY FATHER GOD HIMSELF**, via **King Solomon Spiritual Library**.

When the signal of the information alerts HRM King Solomon David Jesse **ETE** from **I THE FATHER** through the **COMPREHENSIVE MEMORY OF GOD** in Him, at anytime in the day or at night and anywhere, whether on the road or any public place, he will take note of the title of the Revelation Lectures. Sometimes if the location is conducive, lectures can take place immediately. If the location is not conducive, **I THE FATHER GOD** fixes the time for the full Lecture Revelation to take place. Most of the time, some of the Lecture Revelations take about a week, a month or six months and so on, to deliver when **I THE FATHER GOD** brings it back from **HIS SUPREME MEMORY** to HRM King Solomon **ETE**.

Take note that the information of **THE FATHER'S TALK (GOD PRESENT)** is not preaching, or the giving of sermons or shared discussion. **THE FATHER GOD** calls them "***LECTURE***

REVELATIONS", which is a Spiritual Case Study for humankind to improve and have the Higherself Consciousness about himself or herself and their **CREATOR**.

For this reason, every human being that comes across any of the information of the **FATHER'S TALK (GOD PRESENT)** should treat it with utmost and absolute respect and reverence at all times.

HRM King Solomon David Jesse **ETE** is not responsible for **THE FATHER'S TALK (GOD PRESENT)** but **ME, THE FATHER GOD HIMSELF. I, THE ALMIGHTY FATHER** only use Him as a way through, just like a loud speaker from the radio or television receiver.

For this reason, HRM King Solomon David Jesse **ETE** will not be held responsible by anyone who does not understand the contents, the concepts and the principles of **THE FATHER'S TALK (GOD PRESENT)** information in King Solomon Spiritual Library. He will not answer any questions or queries from spirit to soul and the physical truth in connection to the above from the lower mind individuals, persons or groups. However, if you are positive and you have love and are humble, have patience and are peaceful and you want to know and understand more of any part of **THE FATHER'S TALK (GOD PRESENT)**; '**You should use fasting and prayer**' and or if anyone has any questions in good faith, he or she is free to write to HRM King Solomon and **THE FATHER** in him will respond. He will not, and there is no response to any questions, queries and anything negative with the craftiness of the evil minds of humankind.

That is why you should first read seven **FATHER'S TALK (GOD PRESENT)** Lecture Revelations before commenting and

THE FATHER GOD with **HIS SUPREME HOLY SPIRIT OF TRUTH** will bless all those who read and accept this information with good faith through the name and blood of our Lord Jesus Christ, *Amien*.

In the name of our Lord Jesus Christ In the blood of our Lord Jesus Christ Now and forever more, Amen

ESTABLISH MY SPIRITUAL LIBRARY

I THE FATHER GOD ALMIGHTY THE SUPREME WORD OF THE UNIVERSE AM THE SPIRITUAL FOOD TO FEED YOUR SOUL. Therefore, **I** want every family in this world, every home in this world, every office, government offices, monarchies, countries, states, regions, counties, communities, local authority compounds, family homes and everyone and everywhere to collect published copies of **THE EVERLASTING GOSPEL AND THE FATHER'S TALK (GOD PRESENT)** Lecture Revelations of KING SOLOMON SPIRITUAL LIBRARY and establish it physically in your houses. This is so that everybody would have these RECORDS. Go to read the books regularly. Every family should have a Library of **MY INFORMATION CENTRE** for their family members.

Every generation of a particular family should be able to easily go to their family Library of KING SOLOMON SPIRITUAL LIBRARY EVERLASTING GOSPEL and the **FATHER'S TALK (GOD PRESENT) Lecture Revelations** and read the Gospels and Lecture Revelations so that generations upon generations will access their KING SOLOMON SPIRITUAL LIBRARY.

You must all have **THE LIBRARY OF THE FATHER GOD ALMIGHTY** called **KING SOLOMON SPIRITUAL LIBRARY THE FATHER'S TALK (GOD PRESENT) LECTURE REVELATIONS** in your homes and offices. The authorities and individuals concerned must see to that. When you establish your branch of KING SOLOMON SPIRITUAL LIBRARY and have the **EVERLASTING GOSPELS** and the **FATHER'S TALK (GOD PRESENT)** Lecture Revelations then that place is blessed and secured. In the name and Blood of Our Lord Jesus Christ, now and forever more, *Amien*.

THANK YOU FATHER

"THEUNISAL-SUREME SEACELION"
The Universal Supreme Season Celebration

=========

"THEUNI-SUREME WORA THECRO-THEUNISE"
The Universal Supreme Word Almighty
The Creator Of The Universe

==================

WWW.COME4WORD.COM

THE OFFICIAL SITE FOR

==============

EVERLASTING

UNIVERSAL ALL WORD SEASON APPRECIATION CEREMONIAL PROGRAM

==========

=

THE UNIVERSAL SUPREME

ALL WORD

SEASON
CELEBRATION
(GOD PRESENT)
SOMETHING MORE THAN

'GOLD'

THE HEART OF ALL MEN IS

WORD

===================

THE WORD IS THE MAKER, THE SOLE ADMINISTRATOR AND THE CREATOR OF THE UNIVERSE THEREFORE, ALL HUMANKIND ON EARTH MUST APPRECIATE THE WORD IN ALL CAPACITIES FOREVER

==============

FROM EVERY OA OF AO TO AO OF AO (1ˢᵗ OCTOBER TO 10th OCTOBER). YEARLY IS THE UNIVERSAL SUPREME **ALL WORD SEASON** CELEBRATION TO APPRECIATE THE FATHER GOD ALMIGHTY

================

CELEBRATION! CELEBRATION!! **CELEBRATION!!!**

THE UNIVERSAL SUPREME WORD CELEBRATION OF ALL TIME
=======

THE ALMIGHTY FATHER GOD, THE CREATOR OF ALL

THINGS BROTHERHOOD

ORGANISED BY
KING SOLOMON SPIRITUAL LIBRARY

=======

HRM KING SOLOMON DAVID JESSE ETE
INSPIRATIONAL HEAD

IN THE HONOUR OF THE
FATHER GOD THE
CREATOR OF
THE UNIVERSE
THE HOLY SPIRIT OF
TRUTH
AND THE KING OF KINGS
AND THE LORD OF LORDS

==========

THANK YOU FATHER

KING SOLOMON SPIRITUAL LIBRARY

THE GOD ENCYCLOPAEDIA WORD OF INFINITY

============

King Solomon Spiritual Library, God Universal Information Centre
FATHER'S TALK (GOD PRESENT)

WITH LOVE

Covered: **This BOOK,** e-book, software or software's, books, websites, videos, audios, idea or ideas, formula or formulas, manual or instruction manual

... Hereby gives you a non-exclusive license to use the ... (THIS BOOK).

Some of the words here are coded with the (WORD OF SUPER HOLY AND INTELLIGENCE FATHER GOD ALMIGHTY)

Title, ownership rights, and intellectual property rights in and to the Website, Books, E-book, Audios and Videos, Shops and Store – e-Stores, Fundraisings, Celebrations and the Supreme Word Seasons Celebration formulas and arrangements, Positive

Inspiration, HOLY (FATA), FATHER GOD ALMIGHTY POSSESSING SPIRIT in thought, in words and in deed, thinking well, speaking well, hearing well and doing well shall remain in me and in ... The BOOK is protected by international copyright.

FATHER'S TALK (GOD PRESENT)
The message in **THE FATHER'S TALK (GOD PRESENT)** does not challenge any authority as individuals, groups or governments of any land or even any belief of any form. It is rather challenging the truth that is hidden from mankind. Therefore, any spirit, soul or physical human being who decides to challenge this truth shall have himself or herself to blame.

Key A

Any individual that reads any of **THE FATHER'S TALK** (GOD PRESENT) with faith; love and acceptance will experience immediate positive change in his or her life from spirit, soul to physical. If he or she accepts the message then he or she will be free from any evil.

Key B: **PEACE AND LOVE**
If you do not believe the contents of any of **THE FATHER'S TALK (GOD PRESENT),** it is possible through **THE FATHER'S** divine love and peace to simply hand over your copy to a friend or somebody else that would like to keep a copy, or by signing out from any of the websites that connect to **THE FATHER'S TALK (GOD PRESENT)** and KING SOLOMON SPIRITUAL e-LIBRARY

without any evil and negative comments then you are blessed and free.

========

FROM THE DESK OF THE INSPIRATIONAL HEAD

Fees, Prices and Donations; There is no refund on fees, prices or donations since your fees, priced payments or donations are used as a charity contribution to do administrative work of **THE SUPREME WORD**, so please kindly read this first before you decide to involve yourself in any of the under mentioned of HRM King Solomon David Jesse **ETE** universal Inspirational Businesses of (**GOD PRESENT**) in cash, kind and otherwise.

I CAME FROM THE FATHER GOD, WITH THE FATHER GOD, AND BY THE FATHER GOD TO ESTABLISH THE FOLLOWING:

THE FATHER'S TALK (GOD PRESENT), The Spiritual Advice, Healing and Counselling on General Live (The Universal Supreme Spiritual General Hospital), New Songs and Psalms of King David and Solomon, The Word of **GOD** Processing City in Ikot Okwo or e-City online, The Trinity Celebration, "**OUC FUND**", The Universal Bank Account For All Creations, "**ERUFA**" ETE Royal Universal Family, "**THEUNISAL-SUREME SEACELION**" The Universal Supreme Word Season Celebration To Appreciate **THE FATHER GOD ALMIGHTY "THEUNI-SUREME WORA THECRO-THEUNISE" The Universal Supreme Word Almighty, THE CREATOR OF THE UNIVERSE. Therefore** all distributors and contributors should attach and make this information available to all readers, website visitors, distributors, affiliates person/group, celebrant and celebrations centres, supporters and promoters, members, workers and voluntary workers, Ete royal universal palace committee, governments and many other centres as an agreement. Please kindly know that I am not answering to any physical human except **PEACE, UNITY AND LOVE.**

"THEUNISAL-SUREME WORA THECRO-THEUNISE".

I AM IN THE STAGE OF SUPER HOLY AND INTELLIGENT FATHER GOD POSITIVE MADNESS OF THE HOLY SPIRIT OF TRUTH, ENYEN ODUDU ODUDU ODUDU ABASI MI OOO ZIM ZIM ZIM ASSASU, POSITIVE POSITIVE

POSITIVE. UKEMEKE AKA IDIOK UNAM.

Let the peace and blessing of THE HOLY FATHER abide with everyone who corporates with this divine **FATHER'S TALK (GOD PRESENT)**

THANK YOU FATHER
BY
THE HOLY SPIRIT OF
THE FATHER GOD
THROUGH HIS SERVANT
The Senior Christ Servant
HRM King Solomon David Jesse **ETE**
Brotherhood of the
Cross and STAR
Eteroyal Universal family
Ikot Okwo The Great City of Refuge,
Ete Community
Ikot Abasi LGA-543001
Akwa Ibom State Nigeria-W/A
Tel. 08036693841
Email: ksslibrary@eteroyalmail.com

==============

READ AT LEAST SEVEN LECTURE REVELATIONS BEFORE YOU CAN MAKE ANY COMMENTS

In the Name of Our Lord Jesus Christ, In the Blood of Our Lord Jesus Christ, Now and forever more

Everybody should have access to and read at least seven **FATHER'S TALK**

(GOD PRESENT) Lecture Revelations before making any comments about it. If you do not go through at least seven **FATHER'S TALK** Lecture Revelations and you comment, you may make mistakes. And when you make mistakes your blood will be upon you because you would have taken voluntary evolution to misquote **THE FATHER GOD THE CREATOR OF THE UNIVERSE.**

One of **THE FATHER'S TALK** stands for one SPIRIT of GOD, which means that THE **FATHER'S TALK (GOD PRESENT)** Lecture Revelations are witnessed by the Seven SPIRITS of GOD, which **I** use as the Seven Churches of GOD and Seven days of the Week, Seven spirits of Creation in one Supreme energy of **THE FATHER GOD**,

THE SPOKEN WORD therefore,

when you read seven **FATHER'S TALK (GOD PRESENT)** Lecture Revelations then, **I, THE FATHER GOD** will reveal you as a positive person and then you will have a portion in **ME**. And one of **THE FATHER'S TALK (GOD PRESENT)** will have a portion in you. Then you would know that this information came from **THE FATHER GOD. THE FATHER'S**

TALK (GOD PRESENT) is not a mere talk from a man!
  In the Name of Our Lord Jesus Christ, In the Blood of Our Lord Jesus Christ, Now and forever more

INVITATION
====
THE UNIVERSAL SUPREME ACKNOWLEDGEMENT
'THE ONLY SOURCE AND REMEDY

TO END ALL HUMANITY PROBLEMS'
Join me to Celebrate; Acknowledge, Appreciate and give full RECOGNITION to
THE UNIVERSAL SUPREME WORD,
YOUR LIFE FORCE,
THE TOTALITY OF ALL TOTALITIES
YOUR CREATOR,
THE FATHER GOD ALMIGHTY,
THE CREATOR OF THE UNIVERSE

WWW.COME4WORD.COM

Contact EMAIL:
hrmkingsolomon@eteroyalmail.com

THANK YOU FATHER

The title List of some of the
FATHER'S TALK
(GOD PRESENT)

1: THE MANUAL OF THE SPOKEN WORD

2: THE MANUAL OF LIFE

3: INVESTMENT WITH GOD

4: ISO IBOT EDEM IBOT

5: THE CHARACTER OF THE NEW WORLD

6: HELPMANTRANS

7: UNDERSTANDING MY WORD

8: TRUTH, POSITION, POST AND NAME

9: NON STOP BLESSING

10: IMPRESSION

11: STAGES OF EDUCATIONS (SPE, SSE & SUE)

12: THE ENGINEERING OF LIFE

13: THE CONTENT PACKAGE

14: THE BUDGET OF THE NEW WORLD

15: DIVINE ATTENTION

16: THE BABY SPIRIT

17: PROMOTION

18: ADVANCE AND PROGRESSING MIND

19: THE TEMPLE OF THE LIVING GOD

20: I AM OK

21: THE SPIRIT OF TRUTH

22: THE PERFECT PERMANENCY

23: THE FATHER GOD, GOD, GOD THE FATHER

24: HUSBAND, WIFE AND CHILD

25: GOD AND HIS HARBINGER

26: LIFE EVERLASTING

27: POSSESS

28: MY MIND AND MY PLAN

29: AFTER HEART AND AFTER MIND

30: MY DECLARATION & STAND IN BCS

31: BEYOND THE HOPE OF FAITH

32: MENTAL STAIN

33: THE PRINCIPLE OF SELF HOLD

34: <u>THE MASTERSHIP</u>

35: HIDU-CUM

36: THE UNIVERSAL PARENT

37: ADVANCED YOU AND ME

38: THE GREAT UNIVERSAL CHANGE

39: THE PROJECTED MIND
40: INDESTRUCTIBLE BLESSED FIVE STARS

41: ASTROTS, GOD PRESENT I AND MY FATHER

42: SONGS THE COMPLETION

43: THE RIGHT BUTTON

44: AKWA ABASI IBOM- ETE - DIRECTING NDITO AKWA IBOM

45: THE DIGITAL AGE

46: GOD IS OFFICIAL CHAMPION

47: A TRUE WITNESS

48: MYSTERY OF PROCREATION AND BIRTH

49: THE UNIVERSAL UMBRELLA

50: THE FORERUNNER

51: A OF A TO Z (FIRST OF ALL)

52: MAN IN THREE CAPACITIES

53: THE TRUE LIFE OF HOLY SPIRIT PERSONIFIED

54: IN-BETWEEN THE FATHER & THE SON

55: DIVINE ARRANGEMENT & AUTHORITY

56: TWENTY FIRST CENTURY IS NOT FOR SATAN

57: THE SUPREME WORD SEASON CELEBRATION

58: THE MAXIMUM DEITY

59: TRANSFORMER TRANSMITTER AND WAVE

60: THE SUPREME FUTURE

61: THE BYLOVE OF WORD

62: THE SIGNATURE OF THE FATHER GOD

63: THE TWO WAYS

64: <u>THE UNDERSTANDING OF LIFE</u>

65: THE GREATER THAN SOLOMON IS HERE

66: THE CONQUEROR

67: THE SPIRITUAL GENERAL INSPECTOR OF LIFE

68: THE NIGERIA IN THE AFRICA
Part one

69: THE NIGERIA IN THE AFRICA
Part two

70: THE CREATOR AND CREATIONS PART ONE

71: THE CREATOR AND CREATIONS PART TWO

72: THE CREATOR AND CREATIONS PART THREE

73: THE SUPREME TEACHER

74: THE SPIRITUAL COVER

75: THE NIGERIA IN THE AFRICA PART THREE

76: THE SUPREME BELIEVE

77: CAST AND BAN (LECTURE IN LIVERPOOL)

78: LIFE EXTENSION MANUAL

79: THE SPIRITUAL TRAFFIC

80: THE VOICE OF THE CREATOR

81: MY OFFICE

82: LIFE SPIRITUAL FIRE EXTINGUISHER

83: INFORMATION

84: FATHER GOD FINAL ARRANGEMENT

85: THE LOVERS OF CHRIST

86: I LOVE YOU, I LOVE YOU TOO

87: THE UNIVERSAL SUPREME UPDATE

88: THE SUPREME ALTAR

89: THE SOURCE AND DESTINATION

90: A SON LIKE THE FATHER THE KING OF KINGS A ROOTS FROM HEAVEN (NOT THIS TIME AROUND)

91: THE TRUE WITNESS AND THE TRUE SERVANT

92: THE FINAL ARRANGEMENT

93: A TRUE NIGERIAN MAN AND WOMAN

94: EVERYONE MUST PERSONALLY INVOLVE

95: BEWARE

96: ESIEN EMANA AKPAN "THE AFRICAN PROBLEMS"

97: THE SECRET OF THE UNIVERSAL PROBLEMS AND THE REMEDY (MUSLIM AND CHRISTIAN FROM THE SAME PARENT)

98: MMU-UDIM – THE BLESSED MOTHER (ABASI ME UDIM)

99: THINK WELL, SPEAK WELL AND DO WELL

100: THE STAGES OF HOW TO PROCESS THE WORD

101: EVIL STAIN, WHO RUNS AWAY FROM WHO

102: BEYOND HUMAN KNOW PURELY SPIRITUAL

103: THE INSPIRATIONAL WRITER

104: BIAKPAN OBIO AKPAN ABASI (THE NEW JERUSALEM CITY)

105: "OBAMA" THE STRAINTHEN AND THE SPIRIT OF BILL GATE AND MICROSOFT

THANK YOU FATHER

www.ingramcontent.com/pod-product-compliance
Ingram Content Group UK Ltd.
Pitfield, Milton Keynes, MK11 3LW, UK
UKHW041257180426
11947UKWH00008B/532